**Foster-Child
Health Care**

Foster-Child Health Care

Florence Kavaler, M.D.
State University of New York
Downstate Medical Center

Margaret R. Swire
New York Health Research
Associates

LexingtonBooks
D.C. Heath and Company
Lexington, Massachusetts
Toronto

Library of Congress Cataloging in Publication Data

Kavaler, Florence.
  Foster-child health care.

  Includes index.
  1. Child health services—United States. 2. Children—Institutional care—
United States. I. Swire, Margaret R. II. Title. [DNLM: 1. Foster home care.
2. Child health services. WA 320 K21f]
RJ102.K38   1983   362.1'9892   81–47184
ISBN 0–669–04561–6

Copyright © 1983 by D.C. Heath and Company

Published simultaneously in Canada

Printed in the United States of America

International Standard Book Number: 0–669–04561–6

Library of Congress Catalog Card Number: 81–47184

To Carl Schoenberg, M.S.,
Senior Editor, Child Welfare,
for his outstanding contributions
to the field of caring for children
and his encouragement of innovation
and sound professional practices

Contents

Figures and Tables

Foreword

This book documents with care the life circumstances of a group of children in New York City who are totally dependent upon their community for sustenance, care, and nurture. The book reveals a bleak aspect of the systems and agencies that are entrusted to provide health and protective services. Those systems and agencies are not unique for their work on behalf of abused, neglected, and abandoned children. In major respects the provider systems are the same as those that serve all children.

The problems are not unique to New York City, although few other places provide either the concentration of children or the investigative talent to undertake similar studies. Less-complete but nonetheless responsible reports from other parts of the country support and extend findings from New York City. For example, a recent special supplement to the *Sunday Santa Fe Times* carried an account of the health of New Mexico's children (October 10, 1982). That account reports, "At any given time as many as 1,200 children are living in foster homes in New Mexico. One child . . . lived in 14 different foster homes—the average is more than three different homes. These are literally 'Children in Limbo'."

This book will not have served its full potential or have responded to the problems it identifies if it attracts a readership concerned only with the plight of children in foster care. The issues require attention from people who are concerned about the cost and adequacy of health services and the well-being of all children and who ponder our society's prevailing ethics and values. Inadequate response to the findings of this book would be a narrowly focused reform in the interests of children in foster-home care. Those reforms are desperately needed; they require a broader context of concern that can be mustered for yet another subcategory of neglected children.

For more than a decade this country has experienced an erosion in its sense of public responsibility for the well-being of vulnerable people. That erosion became sufficiently complete in the first two years of the Reagan administration to reveal a hard-rock position that made social neglect seem not only an economic necessity but also a Spartan virtue; neglects were made to masquerade as freedoms. Note the degrees of freedom enjoyed by the children described in this book.

Current social policies in this country were put in place acknowledging that anticipated but poorly defined benefits would be much delayed, that in the period of adjustment many people would suffer, and that poor people would suffer most. Little recognition was given to the fact that poor people in this country are predominantly children; more than half the members of poverty-level households are under twenty-one years of age. Poor infants, children, and youth are experiencing reduced services and supports in order to serve a great many other interests including corporate mergers and military preparedness.

At one time national security was defined partially in terms of the health and vigor of children. The preamble to the School Lunch Program opened with, "It is declared to be the policy of Congress, as a measure of national security, to safeguard the health and well-being of the Nation's Children" (U.S. Code 1751, 1946). That emphasis is conspicuously lacking in today's formulations about strategies for protecting the nation's future.

No sound claim can be made that services on behalf of children in this country were once strong and that the present administration has weakened them. Our commitment to children has never been adequate; many children have been deprived persistently of essential services, and other children have been served badly by numerous well-intended but incomplete efforts. Advocacy to improve these circumstances has progressed from time to time with promising programs—for example, Aid for Families with Dependent Children, Head Start, Early Periodic Screening, Diagnosis and Treatment, and the Supplemental Food Program for Women, Infants, and Children. These programs, although much maligned and often attacked, have done much to improve the well-being of children. No one has spoken hopefully of similar new initiatives in recent years. The presumed needs of the marketplace have taken precedence over the needs of children.

Our nation's leaders report that this country faces an economic crisis. We must believe them. However, no leadership yet gives sufficient attention to an even more-alarming problem. We face as a nation an ethical crisis. Unresolved conflict is associated with considerations of social justice and equity, public/private tensions, uses of technology, stereotypes of the family as a social unit, neglects that masquerade as freedoms, accountability and regulation, comprehensive or categorical care, the relationship among different levels of government, environmental protection, and dysjunction between provider wants and public needs. Among the value controversies that immobilize us, no side of any of these causes can make a case so compelling as to justify the failure of this once vigorous and humane nation to protect its most vulnerable people. Around that goal we should make common cause in search of an ethic that overrides our preferences on lesser issues. That higher ethic will require us to achieve favorable health outcomes for children no matter who the providers may be, no matter what the means for their finance, and no matter what the provider system in which they work. These circumstances may well differ from one locale to another, but they cannot be allowed to differ substantially in the health achievements for the populations they serve.

Neither the ethics of the marketplace nor those of a wide array of voluntary community agencies are good enough to resolve this nation's ethical crisis. Present performance and ethics are certainly not good enough to serve the health interests of a large number of neglected children. A higher ethic is required, as this book documents so abundantly.

C. Arden Miller, M.D.
Professor and Chairman,
Department of Maternal and Child Health,
University of North Carolina,
School of Public Health,
Chapel Hill, North Carolina

Acknowledgments

We wish to acknowledge the many individuals and agencies whose contributions made this project possible. Foremost is Margaret Heagarty, M.D., who gave assistance and counsel during all phases of the initial foster-child health-evaluation study while she was director of the Pediatric Outpatient Evaluation Clinic of New York Hospital–Cornell Medical School. Dr. Heagarty made it possible for the study to use the facilities of New York Hospital for the clinical examinations, recruited and supervised the team of physicians and nurses who conducted these pediatric examinations, and guided us in the interpretation of the health data.

A special debt of gratitude is due to Robert Lilienfeld, Ph.D., for his invaluable aid and support in the design phase of the study and in some of the analyses and interpretation of the quantitative data gathered, and to Martin Weitzner, Ph.D., for a variety of consultant services as a social scientist.

The pediatricians, psychiatrists, psychologists, speech and hearing specialists, nurses, and other examiners involved in the clinical survey deserve special recognition for their productive efforts. In addition, special mention is also due other individuals responsible for the collection and tabulation of data; in particular, Joan Krakes for her energy and diligence in supervising the day-to-day clinic activities and Vicki Ellsberg, who put forth much effort in the difficult task of organizing, coding, and editing the data gathered.

The General Policy Advisory Committee and the Study Agency Advisory Committee were supportive and enabling in their insights and practical guidance that increased the opportunities for successful completion of the research endeavor.

The foster-child health-evaluation study was supported by Grant no. MC–R360032–01–0 from the Maternal and Child Health Service, Health Services and Mental Health Administration, U.S. Department of Health, Education, and Welfare, awarded to the New York City Health Department and administered by the Medical and Health Research Association of New York City.

The following New York City Health Department colleagues served as coprincipal investigators for various periods during the evaluation of health services for foster children and should be commended for their efforts to keep the study on track: Lowell E. Bellin, M.D., M.P.H.; Steven Rosenberg, M.D., M.P.H.; Donna O'Hare, M.D.; Margaret Grossi, M.D., M.P.H.; and Melvin Schwartz, M.D., Ph.D.

Although we called upon many physicians and social scientists to advise us on our progress, the primary consultants should be cited: Ernest J. Anastasio, Donald Rubin, Ph.D., and John Barrone, from the Data Analysis Division of the Educational Testing Service (Princeton, N.J.); Ms. Sheila Butler, Speech and Hearing Center, New York Hospital–Cornell Medical School; and Edward L. Greene, M.D., and Joseph H. Herson, M.D., from the Department of Psychiatry, Columbia University College of Physicians and Surgeons.

Research assistants Robert Enteen, Victoria Elsberg, and Gloria Smythe, and the administrative assistant, Patricia Valentine, managed the myriad details of data from the multiple sources, and their work was crucial to the integrity of the project.

Over the years, several analyses were performed on the basic set of data and were reported selectively in separate articles in *Child Welfare* and the *Journal of Health Politics, Policy and Law.* New analyses are presented on original data to form the basis or contribute to the social- and behavioral-science literature of foster care.

For this book as well as the articles, we take full responsibility for the analytic, descriptive, and comparative components as well as the judgments and recommendations that emerge within the text.

The opportunity to share our data, ideas, and social philosophy with concerned professionals in social science and medicine; to inform the curious and interested public; and to stimulate debate and action in the child-health field are the motivations behind this book.

Study Agency
Advisory Committee

Mrs. Jane D. Edwards, executive director, Spence-Chapin Adoption Services;

Mrs. Ruth V. Friedman, director, Salvation Army Foster Home Adoption Service;

Miss Joyce Watts, associate director, Catholic Guardian Society of Brooklyn;

Miss Marie Fitzmaurice, supervisor, Catholic Guardian Society of Brooklyn;

Ms. Mary Nixon, Boarding Home Department, New York Foundling Hospital;

Mr. Irving Rabinow, director, Foster Home Department, Jewish Child Care Association;

Mrs. Louise Pitts, representing Mrs. Dall, director for interagency relationships, New York City Department of Social Services;

Mr. Albert Maloney, director, Queens Boarding Home Office, New York City Department of Social Services;

Mr. Emanuel Fox, deputy director, Direct Care Services, New York City Department of Social Services;

Ms. Joanne Goodman, assistant for Program for the Handicapped, Special Services for Children and Youth/Human Resources Administration.

General Policy
Advisory Committee

Ms. Eulala Steele King, executive associate director, Council of Voluntary Care Agencies;

Ms. Reena Shulman, associate director, Jewish Board of Guardians;

Mr. Irving Rabinow, director, Foster Home Department, Jewish Child Care Association;

Ms. Angela Gentile, program coordinator, New York Catholic Charities;

Ms. Barbara Blum, assistant administrator/commissioner, Special Services for Children and Youth/Human Resources Administration;

Ms. Joanne Goodman, assistant for Programs for the Handicapped, Special Services for Children and Youth/Human Resources Administration;

Mrs. Adolin Dall, director for interagency relations, New York City Department of Social Services;

Mr. Emanuel Fox, deputy director, Direct Care Services, New York City Department of Social Services;

Mrs. Rose Gutman, director, Division of Foster Home Care, New York City Department of Social Services;

Ms. Sylvia Hunter, senior program specialist for health affairs, Human Resources Administration.

1   Introduction

During the past century there has been steadily rising humanitarian concern as well as philosophical interest in the social, emotional, and health needs of children who are placed in foster homes, group homes, or institutions on a temporary or permanent basis. Most recently, however, this concern has been transformed into a vital issue of public policy revolving around the adequacy, efficiency, and cost-effectiveness of present methods of both delivering and paying for various types of services for these children. In the United States, legislation enacted in the last decade has removed some of the financial barriers to the effective provision of health- and medical-care services, especially for children. Conceptual schemes and theoretical frameworks have been formulated and empirical studies have been implemented to assess different aspects of such service. Nonetheless, despite these developments, there are many indications that millions of needy children eligible for free health care in this country have failed to receive adequate levels of preventive or specialty services. Of particular concern are those children who are medically indigent, without homes of their own, and in foster care.[1]

Nearly 500,000 children in this category live in the United States today, with a continuing trend toward an increase in the number of children so placed.[2] Although foster care offers a viable temporary system for providing for children at risk, considerable documentation suggests that this alternative-care mechanism often fails to deliver the necessary services. Thus, although originally conceived to give temporary care to abused, unwanted, or orphaned children, available evidence indicates that foster-care service has evolved over the years into an operation that often keeps these youngsters rootless and uncertain about their futures. It perpetuates their foster-care status by doing little to prevent the collapse of families and very little to find permanent adoptive homes when families collapse. Moreover, all too often foster children become victims of abuse and maltreatment by the very system that seeks to protect them, often leading to deep social and emotional problems.[3] A recent New York City study performed by the staff of the city council found that reported abuse of foster children was more common than among the city's general child population—9.2 per 1,000 foster children compared with 7.5 per 1,000 for the general popula-

1

tion. Moreover, in 1981, 86 cases of abuse were found in private foster homes, and 35 percent of these homes where child abuse occurred remained certified and continued to house children even after the abuse had been found.[4]

Despite these system inadequacies, public expenditures in this area are vast. In 1979, for example, a staggering $2 billion were expended in this country for the provision of child-welfare services. On a per child basis, nationally, current public costs average $3,600 per year per child.[5] In New York City alone, where children spend an average of seven years in foster care, total costs will amount to nearly $250 million, or nearly $40,000 per child.[6] In the area of health care, sharp and rising public expenditures for this Medicaid-eligible population has reached what many consider to be critical levels. During fiscal year 1973–1974 Medicaid funds expended by federal, state, and local governments for health services for these children exceeded $200 million.[7] In New York City for the same time period, Medicaid reimbursement, excluding in- and outpatient costs, exceeded $22 million for the 28,000 children so placed.[8] By 1981, this figure reached $30 million, representing a 36 percent increase in costs despite a 15 percent decline in the number of children served by 1981 ($n = 23,664$).[9] Nationally, the Congressional Budget Office (CBO) estimates a fifteenfold increase in Medicaid expenditures between the period 1967 through 1986.[10]

Such an enormous infusion of public money requires accountability, surveillance, and appraisal of the relative economy and appropriateness of the services rendered. In recognition of this need, the New York City Health Department designed and implemented an investigation to assess the health status and medical-care needs of children in foster boarding-home care and to determine the relationship among the cost of care, the needs of these children, and the structure and functioning of existing health-delivery systems. This effort represented the first systematic attempt by a major city to examine these issues. This book describes the historical events preceding this investigation, the assumptions underlying the methodologic approach, the field procedures, and the findings of the project.

The foster-care situation in New York City is unusually complex and diverse for two primary reasons: (1) the volume of children in care and (2) the manner in which they are served. New York City, with over 23,000 children under public charge within its jurisdiction,[11] has a child-welfare program exceeded in volume by less than a half dozen states in this country. Furthermore, with almost 90 percent of its public charges in voluntary placement of some form, the city relies almost exclusively on the private sector for the provision of such services.[12]

There exists currently in New York City a network of over seventy agencies, administratively autonomous but largely government funded, that provides care to the New York City foster-child population. Whether a child is placed in a boarding home, a group home, an institution, or a residential treatment center, there may be considerable variation in the manner in which his social, emotional, and health needs are met. Organizational patterns and placement policies determine the characteristics of the children in care in different facilities. This is particularly evident with respect to religion; while every agency legally can accept a child of any religion, this is rare. Private-sector facilities often are members of sectarian federations (Catholic Charities, Federation of Jewish Philanthropies, and Federation of Protestant Welfare Agencies), but a smaller fourth group of agencies is not affiliated with any federation and is nonsectarian in auspices and services. To comply with the state constitution, an attempt is made to place each child in a facility of his or her religious persuasion. Since private or voluntary agencies do not have sufficient resources to accommodate all the displaced children, a pool of children is relegated to whatever state or city direct-care facilities are available, but this represents a minority of this population.[13]

The city's reliance on the private sector is not new. In fact, it has strong roots in history. In 1601, an English Poor Law provided the first justification for public intervention for the indigent and orphaned.[14] However, during Colonial times most dependent children were removed from their homes and either placed in unsanitary and overcrowded almshouses alongside the insane, the criminal, and the elderly or, if more fortunate, were placed elsewhere as apprentices or indentured servants.[15] In New York State, in 1811, public aid to private child-care facilities was authorized, but it was not until 1875 that laws were passed requiring the removal of orphaned children from almshouses.[16] Since no alternate public programs existed to care for these children, religious associations and private facilities emerged to serve this population. This situation existed not only in the late nineteenth century but also in the early twentieth century. Public concern, however, did lead to the development of some standards of service for these children. In 1868, Massachusetts was one of the first states to pay families to provide foster homes.[17] In 1909, a White House Conference on the Care of Dependent and Neglected Children supported the notion of aid for dependent families as well as the desirability of home as opposed to institutional care.[18] Although by 1935 nearly all of the states offered Aid for Families with Dependent Children for most of these children, placement and institutionalization continued to occur.[19]

National data show that in 1977, about three-quarters of the 500,000 children in care were in foster boarding homes, representing a threefold rise in the number of children so placed since 1961.[20] Statistics for the years 1933 to 1969 indicate an unbroken and long-term trend toward an increase in the total number of children in foster care.[21] Between 1960 and 1970, the number of children requiring placement in foster-family care rose from

2.4 to 3.8 per 1,000. In some areas in the United States, however, there has been a leveling off.[22] For example, California, which is second to New York State in terms of its foster-care population, has shown a decline in the past few years. In New York State, between 1960 and 1970, there was a 15 percent rise in the number of children in care, followed by a 15.6 percent decline between 1971 and 1974.[23] More recently, the number of children in care in New York State has stabilized at about 50,000.[24] For New York City, an analysis of trends over the past two decades indicates a similar pattern. Thus, between 1960 and 1974, the number of children in care rose from 18,424 to 28,600 followed by a drop to 23,664 in the late 1970s.[25] In addition, since 1960, there has been a gradual rise in the proportion of black and Hispanic foster children with a concomitant decline in the proportion of white children. Whereas blacks comprised 30 percent and Hispanic 20 percent of the children in care in 1960, today together they account for 80 percent of those placed.[26] Since 1971, the number of Hispanic youngsters placed has leveled off whereas the number of black children in care has risen steadily. In addition, there has been a significant drop in the number of preschool children placed in the city, while the proportion of adolescents entering care has more than doubled.[27]

These factors are relevant to our evaluation of agency health programs since they suggest needs and circumstances of identifiable groups of children that are significant for the provision of exemplary health services. Thus, considerable evidence documents the fact that the foster-care system, to a great extent, serves children exhibiting precisely those characteristics that have long been associated with the greatest unmet needs for health services and the poorest availability of these services. One recent study reported that 54 percent of the children in care in New York City came from families dependent on welfare.[28] Another New York City investigation, conducted by Fanshel and Shinn, found that of the 624 children and their families followed over a five-year period, the majority (73 percent) was of racial or ethnic minority status, most of the households were located in impoverished neighborhoods of New York City—neighborhoods supporting numerous real and potential health hazards—over half of these households (52 percent) were receiving some form of public assistance, and only 28 percent of the salary-supported households had weekly incomes above $100.[29] Other studies have substantiated the foregoing findings, supporting the fact that pervasive poverty, financial deprivation, and family disruption are characteristics highly correlated with foster-care placement. [30] A 1978 survey performed by the New York State Temporary Commission on Child Welfare, reported that four out of five children entered care because of parental problems.[31] Moreover, related data indicated that the principal reasons for placement were unwillingness to care for the child or emotional difficulties of the parents, with only a minority placed because of child-related problems or environmental conditions.[32]

Although abundant literature was available in 1971, at the time this study was initiated pertaining to the psychosocial problems and social needs of foster children, only a paucity of published information focused on the health needs of this special population, their health levels, or existing health-care systems.[33] These data were provided principally by a few state and city child-welfare agencies' record surveys of in-house clientele. In 1971 neither pediatric nor public-health journals had focused on this subject. The few clientele surveys that were conducted, however, did provide some insight into the health characteristics of this population by consistently producing data that suggested higher levels of chronic illness and poorer health levels among foster children than among children in the general child population. In one survey undertaken by a New York City voluntary facility, an analysis of the medical records of agency clientele showed that 55.4 percent of those cared for had some form of somatic pathology.[34] In the same year, a different study, performed by the city's Bureau of Child Welfare, found an unusually high level of congenital anomalies, mental retardation, and psychiatric disorders for a sample of 100 children in direct placement with a city facility.[35]

While no attempt has been made to determine the degree of severity of such conditions in either the foster-care or the general child population, it has been estimated that between 20 and 40 percent of all children nationwide suffer from one or more chronic conditions including eye, speech, and orthopedic disorders, as well as emotional disturbances.[36] In terms of children receiving child-welfare services, estimates show that some 1.7 million are mentally retarded, 1.4 million are emotionally disturbed, 700,000 have learning disabilities, and 450,000 are either visually handicapped, deaf, or crippled.[37] Conditions like these represent an important challenge to the medical profession since a chronically ill or handicapped child could suffer the consequences of his or her illness for many years.

With regard to dental care, authors such as Cons and Leatherwood have revealed the disproportionate failure of the children of the poor to utilize routine and therapeutic dental services at an early age.[38] Richmond and Weinberger cite statistics that indicate that 60 percent of children whose family income was less than $2,000 had never been to a dentist, as compared to 10 percent of those whose family income was over $7,000.[39] These figures are particularly significant in view of the fact that children entering foster-care placement derive, for the most part, from a condition of poverty.

Concerning the health of children and youth in general, Richmond and Weinberger, Smith and Gorman, and others have noted the tendency toward lesion-centered rather than preventive pediatrics, as well as the inadequacy of preventive health education.[40] Here, again, children entering foster care are precisely those who are least likely to have received routine preventive care including necessary immunizations prior to placement due to the well-documented lack of health resources available to the poor and the relative lack of health sophistication on the part of the natural parent. Data from an unpublished study of utilization by sixty-one foster-home children in an upstate New York community revealed that physicians were not complying with the state welfare agency's standards of care for frequency and kind of preventive services. The study found that instead, the physicians were "following habit patterns of neglecting to perform and/or record certain parts of the physical examination and only 35 percent of the periodic examinations were complete.[41] Utilization figures reported for immunizations and routine dental care presented an even less-favorable picture than the frequency of physical examinations for these foster children.

In a later investigation in 1970, also unpublished, Koppanyi reported that only three out of twelve social-service facilities representing eleven states and Washington, D.C., exhibited well-planned, well-organized, and centrally coordinated systems of health care for foster children.[42]

Helen Stone of the Child Welfare League of America surveyed a national sample of 336 agencies in 1969 concerning their current practices and attitudes. While discussion of agency medical services is conspicuously absent in this survey, the responses to one survey question revealed that only 7 percent of the local, 13 percent of the state, and 30 percent of the voluntary agencies responding thought that their medical programs were meeting the needs of foster children under their care effectively.[43]

It is recognized universally that the goals of an effective child-health program should include the maintenance and improvement of the well child's present function, treatment and care of the sick child, and methods to ensure the future health of the child. Furthermore, the New York State Department of Social Services has noted that "the quality of the medical program of an institution will depend not only on the high standards of its provision for care, but on the understanding of everyone concerned as to his responsibilities in carrying it out."[44] While numerous standards and guidelines for the content and organization of comprehensive agency child-health programs exist, it is the unfortunate case that many agencies have failed to incorporate these requirements into a formalized, well-functioning, and effective health program.

In fact, in New York City, vast differences are evident with regard to the health-care delivery systems of the social agencies. Though in theory the Medicaid program may insist upon high-quality care, no one standard is used or mandated in the provision of medical services to this foster-care population. Legal guidelines of the New York State Department of Social Services are minimal and provide only general pragmatic supervision.[45] Consequently, agencies are ostensibly free to define the scope, scale, and nature of their services. Program objectives, operations, and outcome vary and may not meet the unique needs of these public charges. Thus, such unevenness may preclude the provision of appropriate social and medical care.

However, with the propitious climate for change and intervention that emerged in the years prior to this survey, federal and state commitments converging on the city provided the opportunity for public-health officials to move beyond their traditionally residual and narrow responsibilities to monitor and evaluate services. With the passage of Title II of the New York State Social Services Law, administrative responsibility for standard setting, surveillance, and enforcement of exemplary publicly funded personal health care was delegated to the New York City Health Department, an agency that actively and successfully exploited its role, having attempted to reduce costs appreciably and to improve the quality of Medicaid professional services.

What does this mean for the 23,000 children in foster placement in New York City who receive medical services through tax-supported funds? Most significantly, it suggests that the health services delivered to such clientele can be appraised and monitored, a process that heretofore has never been sufficiently routine and many sided to be effectively responsive to the needs of these dependent, neglected, and abused children. Pertinent information to accomplish this task focuses on issues and questions such as the following:

Health Needs
1. What are the major health problems characteristic of foster children in New York City?
2. What is the incidence and severity of particular physical and emotional problems?

Health Needs versus Medicaid Costs
1. Do the need levels relate to the cost and scope of services provided?
2. Are health expenditures a function of need?
3. Do children in an agency with high health-care costs need more care than children in an agency with low health-care costs?

Structure of Medical Care versus Costs
1. To what extent do these cost differences reflect specific organizational features of particular agency medical programs, and are these differentials justified?
2. Are particular types of agency medical-care organizations characterized by a higher utilization of costly specialists?
3. What is the relationship between the frequency of medical services provided and cost?

Structure of Medical Care versus Outcome
1. Does the degree of health centralization or decentralization of the organization of a health program relate to current health levels?

2. Do differential health-care-utilization rates result in differential
health levels among agency clientele?

These are complex questions to which no single study could respond in
a definitive manner. Nonetheless, within the methodologic constraints of
the research design in the present investigation, we addressed these concerns
in order to provide data for the development of rational plans for the delivery of optimal services as well as standards for such services.

Notes

1. Foster care refers to the variety of custodial-child welfare services
available to children whose natural families cannot or will not care for them
for a temporary or extended period of time. Services may be provided in a
variety of settings: foster-family homes, group homes for 7 to 8 children,
institutional facilities for as many as 1,000 children, or special residential
treatment centers for the emotionally or physically handicapped.

2. Ann W. Shyne, "Who Are the Children? A National Overview of
Services," *Social Work Research and Abstracts* 16 (Spring 1980):26–33;
and Shyne and Anita G. Schroeder, *National Study of Social Services to
Children and Their Families.* National Center for Child Advocacy, U.S.
Children's Bureau, U.S. Department of Health, Education, and Welfare,
pub. no. (OHDS) 78–30150 (Washington, D.C., August 1978).

3. Alfred Kadushin, "Child Welfare Strategy in the Coming Years:
An Overview," in *Child Welfare Strategy in the Coming Years,* U.S.
Children's Bureau, U.S. Department of Health, Education, and Welfare,
pub. no. (OHDS) 78–30158 (Washington, D.C., p. 35; National Commis-
sion on Children in Need of Parents, "Who Knows? Who Cares? Forgotten
Children in Foster Care" (New York: Child Welfare League, 1979), pp.
5–7; U.S., Congress, Senate, Subcommittee on Children; House, Select
Subcommittee on Education, *Hearings on Foster Care,* December 4, 1975;
"State Foster Care Termed a Failure at Hearing," *The New York Times,*
March 21, 1982; and J. Knitzer and M.L. Allen, *Children without Homes*
(Washington, D.C.: Children's Defense Fund, 1978).

4. "City Planning Changes in Bid to Stem Abuse in Foster Homes,"
The New York Times, August 15, 1982.

5. National Commission on Children in Need of Parents, "Who
Knows?" pp. 5–7.

6. "City Council President's Adoption Research Project," mimeographed (New York, December 1980).

7. U.S. Department of Health, Education, and Welfare, *Medical
Assistance (Medicaid) Financed under Title XIX of the Social Security Act,*
DHEW pub. no. (SRS) 75–03150 (Washington, D.C., January 1974).

8. New York State Department of Social Services, *Statistical Report on Vendor Medical Care,* no. Department of Social Services–719 (Albany, N.Y., 1974); and New York City Department of Social Services, "Summary Analysis of Monthly Population Reports Submitted by Foster Care Agencies: Children Remaining in Care," mimeographed (New York, June 30, 1974).

9. New York State Department of Social Services, "Medical per Diem Rates for Child-caring Agencies and Institutions," mimeographed (Albany, N.Y.: Division of Medical Assistance, 1981); and Child Welfare Information Services, "Summary of Characteristics of Children in Care or Recently Discharged," mimeographed (New York, March 31, 1981).

10. "Study Cites Soaring Medicaid Costs and Uneven Eligibility Standards," *The New York Times,* June 23, 1981; and Executive Office of the President, *The Budget of the United States Government. Fiscal Year, 1981* (Washington, D.C.: Office of Management and Budget, 1981).

11. Child Welfare Information Services, "Summary of Characteristics."

12. Foster care at public charge refers to those children in any type of foster-care placement in (1) a voluntary or private agency for whom the New York City Bureau of Child Welfare has authorized a payment of public funds or (2) one of the programs operated by the bureau. Recent figures indicate that in New York City, 97 percent of all children in care are charges as defined here; only 3 percent of all children in placement have the full cost of their care paid for by their families or other private funds. Of the public charges, 14 percent receive care in publicly owned and operated facilities. Thus, the city purchases 86 percent of the required foster-care placements from independent private agencies. The authority and responsibility for care remains, however, with the public agency. Hence, an extraordinary degree of coordination is required between the large network of private agencies and the small group of public facilities providing direct services. See U.S. Department of Health, Education, and Welfare, *Child Statistics,* DHEW pub. no. (SRS) 73-03258, NCSS Report E-9 (Washington, D.C., March 1971).

13. New York City Department of Social Services, "Summary Analysis."

14. R.H. Brenner, *Children and Youth in America: A Documentary History* (Cambridge, Mass.: Harvard University Press, 1971), vol. 1, pp. 64, 631–633; vol. 2, pp. 291–293, 322–323.

15. Ibid.

16. Justine Wise Polier, *Everyone's Children, Nobody's Child* (New York: Charles Scribner's Sons, 1941), p. 214, as cited in City of New York Human Resources Administration, *Legislative Review: Social Services Legislation and Action,* Winter 1975, p. 4.

17. Brenner, *Children and Youth in America.*

18. *Proceedings of the Conference on the Care of Dependent Children* (Washington, D.C.: Government Printing Office, 1909), p. 18.

19. Brenner, *Children and Youth in America;* and G. Abbott, *The Child and the State,* vol. 2 (Chicago: University of Chicago Press, 1938), pp. 229–331.

20. Shyne, "Who are the Children?"

21. U.S. Department of Health, Education, and Welfare, *Child Statistics.*

22. Kadushin, "Child Welfare Strategy in the Coming Years," p. 58.

23. Trude Lash and Heidi Sigal, *The Status of the Child* (New York, 1976).

24. Virginia Hayes Gibbison and John M. McGowan, "New York State Children in Foster Care Executive Summary," Welfare Research, Inc., 1977.

25. Lash and Sigal, *The Status of the Child.*

26. Ibid.

27. Blanche Bernstein, Donald A. Snider, and William Meezen, *Foster Care Needs and Alternatives to Placement: A Projection for 1975 to 1985* (New York State Board of Social Welfare, 1975).

28. George Strauss, *The Children Are Waiting: The Failure to Achieve Permanence for Foster Care Children in New York City* (New York City Comptroller's Office, 1977).

29. David Fanshel, "The Exit of Children from Foster Care," *Child Welfare,* no. 2 (1971):80.

30. Henry S. Maas and Richard E. Engler, *Children in Need of Parents* (New York: Columbia University Press, 1959); Lucille J. Grow and Ann W. Shyne, *Requests for Child Welfare Service* (New York: Child Welfare League of America, 1969); Shirley Jenkins and Elaine Norman, "Families of Children in Foster Care," *Children* 16 (1969):4; Mignon Sauber, "Pre-placement Situations of Families: Data for Planning Services," *Child Welfare* 46 (December 1967):10; and Helen R. Jeter, *Children, Problems and Services in Child Welfare Programs* (Washington, D.C.: U.S. Children's Bureau, 1963).

31. Joseph Pisani, *Foster Care Reimbursement: A New Approach* (Temporary State Commission on Child Welfare, 1978).

32. Bernstein et al., *Foster Care Needs;* Maas and Engler, *Children in Need of Parents;* and Mary Ann Jones et al., *A Second Chance for Families: Evaluation of a Program to Reduce Foster Care* (New York: Child Welfare League of America Research Center, 1978).

33. D. Fanshel, "The Pediatrician and Children in Foster Care," *Pediatrics* 60 (1957):255; Committee on Adoption and Dependent Care, "Health Needs of the Child in Foster Family Care," *Pediatrics* 59 (1977):465; and Committee on Adoption and Dependent Care, "The Needs of Foster Children," *Pediatrics* 56 (1975):144.

34. Harold Goldstein, M.D., "Medical Diagnosis" (New York: Report of the Jewish Child Care Association, 1965).

35. Margaret Grossi, M.D., "Survey of Medical Services of the Bureau of Child Welfare, Division of Foster Home Care" (Report to the New York City Department of Health, July 1965).

36. J.B. Richmond and H.L. Weinberger, "Program Implications of New Knowledge Regarding the Physical, Intellectual, and Emotional Growth and Development and the Unmet Needs of Children and Youth," *American Journal of Public Health, Conference on Health Services for Children and Youth* 60 (New York, April 1970).

37. Kadushin, "Child Welfare Strategy."

38. Naham C. Cons and Ernest C. Leatherwood, Jr., "Dental Services in Community Child Health Programs," *Amercian Journal of Public Health* 60 (July 1970):1245–1249.

39. Richmond and Weinberger, "Program Implications."

40. Richmond and Weinberger, "Program Implementation;" and Donald C. Smith, M.D., and Gwen C. Gorman, "Health Supervision of Children in Foster Care," *Child Welfare,* March 1960.

41. A.S. Yerby, Margaret M. O'Neill, and Stella M. Dorsey, "Utilization of Child Health Services by Children Placed in Direct Foster Care and in Receipt of ADC and Home Relief" (Albany: New York State Department of Social Welfare).

42. Z. Koppanyi, unpublished study, 1970.

43. Helen D. Stone, *Reflections on Foster Care: A Report of a National Survey of Attitudes and Practices* (New York: Child Welfare League of America, 1969).

44. New York State Department of Social Services, *Rules and Recommendations for Child-Caring Institutions,* pub. 1064 (Albany, N.Y., May 1969).

45. Ibid.

2 General Plan and Research Procedures

This chapter describes the underlying assumptions of the research plan, the basic strategy, the sampling procedure, the health examination, and other field procedures carried out during this investigation. Though the original set of specifications required some minor modifications, the basic design remains the same as initially conceived.

Approach

Any research relating to evaluating, planning, or strengthening organizational and delivery systems must, of necessity, be based on certain assumptions, some widely held, others more personal and restricted. The assumptions involved in the conduct of our foster-care study and against which service systems were assessed are outlined in the following paragraphs.

1. The social agency is ultimately responsible for the medical management of children under its care, a fundamental component of the child's total care. As such, the agency should provide all the personal-health services for which it is accountable. This includes preventive and comprehensive care, the former being the core of service in that raising the quality of such periodic supervision will in effect reduce the amount of interventive care. Inherent in this concept is the notion that children require and profit from regular medical supervision when they are free from illness as well as when they are ill. The commitment to dispense such care requires that the agency have a definite plan, clearly defined policies, trained professional staff, and appropriate facilities. Without such a systematic program for medical services, the agency would abrogate its responsibility for control of care and would compromise its function.

2. Competent administration of the medical program of a social agency requires the professional direction of a qualified pediatrician, who will supervise and integrate the services as well as assure their appropriate health content through the formulation of explicit policies and procedures.

Implicit in this role is the responsibility for selection, approval, and supervision of qualified and competent primary physicians and specialists who will be responsive to the concept of accountability. Local practitioners,

13

if utilized for their accessibility, should constitute a panel and should have a thorough understanding of the program as well as of the concept of control—namely, the agency's need to review and monitor services rendered periodically.

An operational program further requires the support of nursing personnel to assist the director and staff pediatricians in effective coordination of each child's care in making referrals, reviewing treatment reports, following the patient during hospitalization, and performing those activities required of a primary medical resource.

3. Comprehensive services are intrinsic to optimum health care. This concept connotes a spectrum of medical and ancillary services encompassing preventive, therapeutic, and rehabilitative services. A plan for provision of care and treatment must be delineated and should include periodic diagnostic appraisal of the child's health; immunizations and tests; specialized clinical services such as dental, eye and ear, psychological and psychiatric, laboratory, X-ray, and other ancillary services; supervision of nutritional needs; and counseling and education of foster parents. Comprehensive care further recognizes the importance of periodic health evaluations for those caring for foster children—the agency staff members as well as foster parents.

4. Accessible service, given adequate central agency control, is indispensable to a flexible and responsive system of care. The sources of care utilized should be reasonably near the foster-family home because the location and not only the nature of services profoundly influence the degree to which service needs are met. Moreover, the option to secure local episodic care during emergencies, accidents, or acute illness should be open.

5. Continuity in the flow of services and personalized care can be assured only if treatment is rendered by the same group of health professionals over an extended period of time. Thus, the organization and staffing of the medical program shall be appropriate to its function with administrative responsibility clearly allocated. The scope and level of care to be provided shall be explicated specifically so they can serve as guidelines for continuous and acceptable service.

Though the value of a child's receiving all health services from a single source is acknowledged, in some circumstances the single source may function more as a coordinator of services than as sole purveyor of care. It is, nevertheless, incumbent on the agency to maintain a continuous relationship with the child, assuring a familiarity with the child's past history and episodes of illness; periodically evaluating his present physical, emotional, and psychological status; and providing services as needed.

The concept of continuity further connotes ongoing direct communication between various sources of care—that is, follow-up of referral appointments, laboratory and X-ray procedures, and other ancillary services. Each functional-area professional involved—for example, dental and mental health—must make his or her findings known to the other involved providers. Only such an approach will lead to the smooth coordination of health services that in turn will elevate the quality of care provided. Moreover, continuity should facilitate follow-up and medical control and make reporting uniform and manageable between the agency medical staff and independent physicians, clinics, and health centers.

6. A continuous and chronological medical record for each child under care shall be maintained by the social agency. This record shall be centrally located and available to attending staff physicians and other health professionals. To assure coherent and complete care, the record shall comprise the child's medical history, preventive and therapeutic treatments, specialty services, laboratory and X-ray reports, episodes of acute illness, as well as dental and mental-health services. Consistent with the concept of accountability, one person shall be in charge of the records and shall be responsible for reports contained therein. Lack of a systematic record system will vitiate an otherwise effective program.

Further, a system of exchange between the agency, local physicians, and hospitals should be worked out, with the responsibility for transferring reports and information from laboratories and specialty clinics to the child's chart clearly designated. A standard procedure for referrals and exchange of information with which staff are familiar inevitably will avoid delay and will facilitate effective, prompt care.

7. Periodic re-evaluation of program objectives and their implementation is the optimum way to elevate care. This, together with a concurrent emphasis on feedback, quality control, and monitoring activities—that is, professional review of reports to assure appropriate service and case accountability—will generate a total balanced system of care, flexible and responsive to the needs of the agency's clientele.

Data Collection

While several conceptual frameworks for appraising medical effectiveness exist, in this study, we used Donabedian's tripartite schema for the assessment of medical-care systems.[1] In his model, health-service variables are classified as the following:

Structure: Organization, record system, payment mechanisms, expenditures;

Process: Conduct of professional staff; diagnostic, preventive, and treatment procedures; follow-up and referral practices;

Outcome: Health status of recipients, health benefit.

The basic assumption underlying this schema is that each of these components of medical practice must be examined to assess the quality of care adequately. Thus, while outcome (that is, end result of medical care, impact of services on the health of patient) commonly has been considered the ultimate test of the efficacy of care, when used as the sole criterion in evaluation it has distinct limitations. The same may be said for process and structure variables. Taken together, however, these elements of medical care can more accurately and adquately illuminate the nature and level of services provided in medical settings.

The research tools employed to gather data pertaining to the structure, process, and outcome of medical care were the medical audit and the direct clinical examination.

The Medical Audit

Defined as the evaluation of medical care in retrospect through the analysis of clinical records, this technique typically involves a comparative appraisal of the recorded process of care with generally accepted standards of care. In his extensive review, Donabedian states that "appropriate recording is itself an important dimension of the qualtiy of care . . . the record is the major vehicle for the coordination of care . . . and for continuity of care."[2]

Although objections have been raised to the use of the medical record as an evaluative tool, an impressive convergence of research findings concludes that good recording does relate to good medical practice and that the relationship, while not perfect, is statistically significant.[3] These findings, taken together with the usually wide acceptance and successful use of this technique, formed the basis for its inclusion in this book.

The instrument used for this investigation was designed to identify the pattern, completeness, and adequacy of preventive, diagnostic, and treatment services as well as to provide a profile of each child's medical history. Process measures incorporated in this instrument included the frequency and completeness of health-maintenance visits, immunization, laboratory and sensory screening status, problem recognition, and follow-up practices. Measures used to delineate the health of the child comprise acute and/or specialty visits, hospitalizations, and diagnosed adverse health conditions. To ascertain the effect of organization on the level of service rendered, providers of care and sites of service also were identified.

Final determination of items for inclusion in the form was made only after widespread consultation with individuals in the field of pediatrics and medical-care evaluation.

A team of six nonphysicians was engaged to perform these audits—a decision supported by the work of other investigators who found audits by lay personnel to be reasonably reliable and most efficient in terms of time and cost.[4] By January 1973, recruitment was completed, and the orientation and training process had begun. Manuals containing precise definitions of each item on the audit form were furnished to the reviewers for training and ongoing reference purposes. Working under the supervision of a staff public-health nurse, the activities of the team were monitored closely throughout this data-collection phase. Reproducibility and reliability of the data were established by having pairs of reviewers, working independently, audit the same records. In all, ninety-five replications were performed. The results, analyzed by enumerating the items coded differently by each pair of reviewers, revealed good agreement among the group. The reviews of agency records were performed between March and October 1973. During the period of field work, audits were completed approximately two weeks prior to the scheduled clinical examinations. Portions of the data that pertained to medical histories then were abstracted and incorporated into the clinical-examination protocol for use by the study pediatricians.

Direct Clinical Examinations

The assumption underlying this approach was that direct clinical-screening examinations provided tests for viewing health and care, as well as a strategy for assessing delivery systems. Clinical examinations were designed to provide a comprehensive impression of the physical, dental, and mental-health status and needs of the study children. In effect, the findings of this clinical survey were to provide baseline data on the physical, psychological, and psychiatric status of these children.

Logistics. Arrangements were made to conduct the examinations at the pediatric outpatient-evaluation clinic of New York Hospital. Clinical sessions commenced in March 1973 and continued through November 1973. The schedule, which called for five days of testing per week, was adhered to closely, with approximately six children seen during each session.

The scheduling process involved the initial mailing of a letter describing the nature and purpose of the examination, a follow-up phone call to set a specific date, and a final reminder slip indicating the appointment time. To minimize the chances that a child would not appear, the study contracted with a car service for the provision of transportation to and from the clinic.

Nature of the Examination. The basic components of the health evaluation, the age ranges for each group of procedures, and the time allotments are shown in table 2-1. Children six years and older required about three

Table 2-1
Components of the Health Examination

Components	Time (In Minutes)	Age Range (In Years)
Pediatric	30	(1–15)
Laboratory tests	15	(1–15)
Vision	15	(over 3)
Audiometric	15	(over 3)
Dental	15	(over 3)
Developmental	30	(under 6)
Psychological	30	(5–15)
Psychiatric	60	(over 6)

hours per examination, and younger children required slightly less time. Since arrival times were similar, it was necessary to vary the sequence of the assessment process for each examinee.

Protocols for the pediatric, vision, audiometric, dental, and mental-health tests were developed with the assistance of consultants.

Pediatric examinations were performed by eight senior resident and attending pediatricians under the supervision of Dr. Margaret Heagarty, director of the Pediatric Outpatient Department, New York Hospital. Orientation to specific study procedures was provided to ensure comparability in performance, with clinical terms and recording procedures defined in detail in a manual prepared for use by the study physicians.

The basic elements of the assessment included an eye, ear, nose, and throat examination; musculoskeletal and neurological evaluations; and a cardiovascular examination. A general inspection for observable deformities, mannerisms, nutritional status, and general appearance was also accomplished. In addition, medical histories (collected from the record survey) were reviewed, and foster mothers were questioned briefly.

To minimize interexaminer bias, the group to be examined was distributed equally among the study physicians. At the completion of each evaluation, the physician made a summary consisting of a clinical impression of the child's basic health and recommendations for referral for subsequent treatment. This summary statement was incorporated into a report of findings sent to each child's agency.

Laboratory tests and body measurements were carried out by a team of New York Hospital nurses and ancillary staff. The specific assessments included recordings of height, weight, and head circumference (up to one and one-half years) and screening for sickle-cell anemia (black children only), tuberculosis, renal disease, and lead poisoning as appropriate for age. A hemoglobin less than 11 grams/100 milliliters and a lead level exceeding 0.06 micrograms/milliliter were considered positive findings requiring further diagnostic workup.

Vision screening for corrected and uncorrected acuity at near and far distances was performed with the Titmas Optical Screener. The examination was made without glasses, and appropriate parts were repeated if the examinee wore glasses and brought them with him/her to the clinic. *The Reference Manual: Titmas Vision Tester* served as a guide for the nurse who performed these tests.[5]

Audiometric testing was accomplished by three audiologists from the staff of the Speech and Hearing Center, New York Hospital. Pure-tone hearing screening was done at test frequencies of 500, 1,000, 2,000, 4,000, and 6,000. The screening level chosen for the study was 20 decibels. For purposes of referral, the fail criterion was no response at one or more test tones in either ear, after two screenings.

Dental examination was designed to provide an objective assessment of the condition of each tooth as well as a determination of the oral-hygiene status of each child. The two indexes employed for this purpose were the DMF (decayed, missing, and filled teeth) scale, developed by Klein et al. of the U.S. Public Health Service,[6] and the OHI–S (Greene and Vermillion's Simplified Oral Hygiene Index),[7] which assesses the amount of debris and calculus on six surfaces. Findings were derived on a uniform basis through the use of written objective standards developed with the assistance of Morton Fisher, D.D.S., of the New York City Health Department and director of the Medicaid Dental Program. These standards, which were followed closely by the study's dental examiners (two New York Hospital interns), served to narrow the range of examiner variability by eliminating many borderline or questionable problems.

Developmental evaluations were made of infants and children under six years of age who were screened for developmental delays and/or retardation (gross motor, fine motor adaptive, language, or person-social) through the Denver Developmental Screening Test (DDST).[8] Selection of the instrument was based on its ease of administration and scoring, its high test-retest reliability (95.8 percent), its high interexaminer reliability (90 percent), and its validation with the Revised Yale Developmental Schedule ($r = .97$).[9] Evaluations were performed by three clinical-developmental graduate students enrolled in American Psychological Association-approved doctoral programs. Orientation and training was provided by a New York Hospital nurse experienced in the administration of this procedure, and the DDST manual served as a teaching instrument and a guide for ongoing reference purposes.

Verbal and nonverbal measures of intellectual maturity were administered by the three clinical and developmental doctoral students and included the Goodenough-Harris Drawing Test. This test was selected because it provides an efficient (ten-to-fifteen-minute administration), reliable (test-retest = .94; split-half = .77), and valid (.76 with Stanford-Binet) nonlanguage measure of mental maturity.[10] In addition, its use permits comparison with nationwide data from the U.S. Health Examination Survey (HES). The standardized instructions as outlined by Harris and as followed by the U.S. Health Examination Survey (Cycle 11) were adhered to in the current study.[11] The Peabody Picture Vocabulary Test (PPVT) also was incorporated in the clinic survey in order to secure a verbal appraisal of mental maturity. Selection of the instrument was based on its efficiency (ten-minute administration), reliability (test-retest = .57–.87), and validity (.83 with Stanford-Binet).[12] The standardized procedures for the administration and scoring of this test as detailed in the PPVT manual were followed closely by the study examiners.

Psychiatric evaluations were completed for a randomly selected subsample of children over six years of age and were performed by a team of psychiatrists trained in the administration of a standardized protocol (that is, screening questionnaire) developed by Thomas Langner and his associates.[13] Recruitment, initial training, and ongoing supervision was accomplished with the assistance of two members of the Langner team, Dr. Edward Greene and Dr. Joseph Herson. The evaluation, which required about one hour to perform, included questions concerning the child's functioning in school, at home, and with his peers; his dreams and fantasies; a brief neurological examination; and an appraisal by the Bender-Gestalt Test. After each interview, the psychiatrist then assigned the child a general rating of impairment and ratings in ten areas of impairment, each on a five-point scale (well-to-minimal, mild, moderate, marked, and severe-to-incapacitated); a so-called caseness rating (an estimate of the psychiatrist's confidence that there should be some form of therapeutic intervention); and a diagnostic impression.

Clinical-Survey Follow-up. Agencies received immediate notification when acute infections were uncovered during the testing sessions, and when indicated, treatment was provided at the clinic. In addition, both normal and abnormal examination results were reported to the agencies.

Supplemental Data

Supplemental data to the examination and the medical audit were gathered for various purposes that can be grouped into the following categories:

Baseline data: To provide a demographic framework against which the examination and record-review findings could be viewed, a questionnaire was designed to collect information on the age, sex, and race of the study child and on his natural and foster family. In addition, income level, household composition, and child-placement data were to be secured through the use of these forms. Access to the social records (the source of these data) by project reviewers was limited to four of the study agencies because of varying policies concerning record accessibility. In the remaining facilities, agency social workers completed these baseline data forms.

Foster-family data: To describe foster-family situations, data were gathered through the use of the baseline-data forms. In addition, personal interviews were conducted with a randomly selected subsample of foster mothers at the examination center by a team of three trained project interviewers. Information was gathered concerning the mother's opinion of the agency medical program, the availability and accessibility of services, and the state of her and her foster child's health. Interviewers were supervised and monitored throughout the data-collection phase by the project administrator and the study's clinic coordinator.

Agency-level resource data: To secure information concerning medical costs, staffing patterns, clinic schedules, and allocation of resources, data were obtained during developmental-year site visits to the facilities of each study agency. Updated information was also obtained during the 1973–1974 clinical-examination phase of the project.

Because of the complexities of the tasks involved in the research design, each study agency appointed a liaison worker to coordinate the collection of data with project staff and to ensure the cooperation of all concerned agency personnel. In addition, two advisory groups composed of professionals in the field of child welfare and administrators of the sampled agencies provided technical assistance and policy guidance.

Sample Design

Selection of Agency Sample

The scope of the sampling plan was dictated by both systematic and expedient factors: (1) the conditions and constraints of New York City's prevailing foster-care system, (2) cost and logistical considerations, (3) statistical factors (it was determined that a child sample of no less than eighty cases per agency was required since a smaller number would reduce seriously our chances of describing and analyzing differences that might have significance for the provision of health services for this group of children), and (4) selected criteria (listed in the next paragraph) that maximized our opportunities for meeting the objectives of this study.

Based upon these considerations, and guided by our general-policy advisory committee, it was determined that a pool of eight agencies could be studied effectively. Two facilities—those that administered the city's direct-care program for some 4,000 children (in 1972, the time the sample was selected)—were, at the recommendation of the advisory committee, given a priority inclusion in the sample.[14] The remaining six agencies were drawn from the pool of fourteen voluntary child-care agencies studied during our developmental-year survey with selection based upon the following criteria: religious auspices, annual Medicaid per capita costs, structure of the medical-care delivery system (centralized versus decentralized), size of foster boarding-home case load, and case load demographic characteristics.

The basis for this approach was the varying nature of the voluntary agencies with respect to these dimensions. Thus, our developmental survey revealed that annual Medicaid per capita costs ranged from a low of $119 to a high of $733 among the voluntary agencies studied. Further, little or no uniformity was evident with respect to the staffing and organization of their health programs, and differences were observed in the degree to which they administratively emphasized the centralization or decentralization of services. These were not mutually exclusive tendencies, however. At best, these agencies could be described as inclined more toward one than the other organizational form, and it was assumed that this might have consequences for the medical care provided to these children. Accordingly, the purpose of our selection approach was to secure significant variation with respect to these dimensions.

In step 1 of our selection procedure, the fourteen agencies studied during the developmental year were classified first by religious auspices— namely, Protestant, Catholic, and Jewish. Then, within, these three groupings, agencies with the lowest and highest Medicaid per capita costs were selected.

Religion	Agency	Per Capita Cost
Protestant	C (five)	Lowest, $137
	M —	Highest, $381
Catholic	K (six)	Lowest, $119
	B (two)	Highest, $497
Jewish	N —	Lowest, $319
	J (one)	Highest, $733

The agencies are identified by letter, as they were during the developmental year; the agencies included in the final analysis are also identified by number consistent with the tables appearing in later chapters.

In step 2, the resultant agencies were inspected with regard to case-load-size representation, as follows:

Size	Agency	n
Large	C (five)	1,188
	B (two)	1,615
Medium	J (one)	498
	K (six)	487
Small	M	248
	N	194

The dimension of agency philosophy and policy regarding the delivery of medical-care services is reflected in their per capita costs by site of service (that is, centralized versus decentralized medical-care delivery systems). In step 3, the foregoing six agencies were classified as follows:

Agency	Per Capita Medicaid Cost for Centralized Services	Decentralized Services
J (one)	$498	$235
N —	281	38
M —	314	67
B (two)	257	240
K (six)	53	66
C (five)	48	89

These cost figures derive from annual reports of medical expenditures submitted by study agencies to the New York State Department of Social Services for the year ending June 30, 1971. These per capita costs include in-house medical costs as well as the cost of services purchased in the community. Excluded are costs for inpatient and outpatient hospital care, which are paid for directly by the Division of Medical Payments of the New York City Department of Social Services.

In step 4, case-load demographic characteristics—that is, ethnicity, age, and religion—were examined with respect to representativeness. All of the foregoing agencies but agency N were found acceptable. This agency, which was one of the two Jewish facilities studied during the developmental year, was dropped from consideration because 84 percent of its case-load consisted of infants under two years of age, a range too narrow for medical and statistical purposes. Inasmuch as no other Jewish agency was available for study from the developmental-survey group, the replacement for agency N derived from the remaining pool of Protestant and Catholic facilities: A, D, E, F, G, H, I, and L. Examination of available data pertaining to these agencies resulted in the selection of agency A, a Catholic facility with a centralized-care system. The other agencies were dropped from consideration for the following reasons:

Agencies E, F, G, and L had substantial numbers of children residing in homes beyond the geographic bounds of the study (ranging from 30 to 95 percent of total homes).

Agency D was not well represented in the under-two-year age category (only 6 percent of its case load was in this age group).

Agency H had annual Medicaid per capita costs ($123) that were comparable to those of another Catholic facility ($119) already in the sample.

Agency I, a Protestant facility, was chosen to replace agency M, another Protestant facility, which was dropped from consideration at the request of its administrative staff because they could not contribute the time that would be required to coordinate the collection of data.

Thus, the final universe of agencies selected for study consisted of two public and six voluntary facilities. These agencies were ranked by Medicaid per capita cost, and in view of its significance for this study, they henceforth are referred to by their numerical position in the following ranking:

Agency Rank by Cost	Developmental-Study Label	Medicaid per Capita Cost
One	J	$733
Two	B	497
Three	I	237
Four	A	181
Five	C	137
Six	K	119
Seven	NYC direct-care facility A	83
Eight	NYC direct-care facility B	83

As noted earlier, the cost figures for the voluntary agencies derive from the annual reports they submitted to the New York State Department of Social Services for the year ending June 30, 1971. Public-agency cost data were supplied by the Bureau of Child Welfare of the New York City Department of Social Services. Since the NYC direct-care facility A maintains their accounting records on a calendar-year basis, their costs are for the year ending December 1971. The NYC direct-care facility B, conversely, has a fiscal-year accounting system. Their cost figures, therefore, are consistent with those of the voluntary agencies.

The following sections and table 2–2 provide a brief description of these agencies.

Agency One. Four-hundred and seventy-eight foster boarding-home children were under the care of this agency as of July 1972. The majority of these children was Jewish (82 percent) and white (73 percent), 17 percent were Protestant, and 23 percent were black. Only 3 percent were Puerto Rican. The medical-care organization featured a part-time medical director, three associate pediatricians, five registered nurses, and one part-time and two full-time secretaries, with a central-headquarters clinic open three afternoons, one morning, and one evening a week. Central-office mental-health specialists included three full-time and ten part-time psychiatrists and two full-fime and four part-time psychologists. In addition, consultants in the areas of cardiology, ophthalmology, and orthopedics were available to the central office. Community affiliates comprised twenty-three ophthalmologists, four orthopedists, and four dermatologists. In terms of costs, services rendered by these professionals totaled $733/child/year for the fiscal year ending June 30, 1971. More than half of these expenditures reflect mental-health costs, about two-fifths are medical and 5 percent are dental costs. Additionally, almost three-fourths of the total expenditures represents care provided by in-house staff.

Agency Two. This agency, under Catholic auspices, served 1,587 children at the time of sample selection. Almost all were Catholic (1,583), more than half were Puerto Rican, 30 percent were white, and 18 percent were black. Medical services for these children reportedly were delivered through facilities at the central office and in suburban counties. The staff featured a part-time medical director, four part-time staff pediatricians, five full-time registered nurses, and three part-time licensed practical nurses. Specialists included three psychiatrists and three psychologists, two ophthalmologists, one radiologist, and one pathologist, all part-time. In addition, community resources reportedly were used as needed. Dental services, though centrally coordinated, were decentrally provided. With respect to cost, the average amount expended per child for the fiscal year ending 1971 was $497.

Table 2–2
Selected Characteristics of Study Sample, by Agency

	Agency							
	One	*Two*	*Three*	*Four*	*Five*	*Six*	*Seven*	*Eight*
Annual per capita medical costs[a]								
Total	$733	$497	$237	$181	$137	$119	$83	$83
Medical	315	396	118	129	96	48	44	28
Dental	32	21	34	20	12	15	10	20
Mental health	386	80	85	32	29	56	30	35
Case load[b]								
Total number	977	1,926	669	2,162	1,199	485	1,729	1,298
Foster boarding home								
Number (Percent)	478 (100)	1,587 (100)	535 (100)	2,136 (100)	1,199 (100)	485 (100)	1,698 (100)	1,298 (100)
Ethnic group								
White								
Number (Percent)	352 (73)	481 (30)	38 (7)	1,083 (51)	52 (4)	187 (39)	126 (7)	104 (8)
Black								
Number (Percent)	109 (23)	281 (18)	497 (93)	473 (22)	1,125 (94)	108 (22)	1,379 (81)	1,154 (89)
Puerto Rican								
Number (Percent)	13 (3)	825 (52)	— (—)	568 (27)	20 (2)	186 (38)	191 (11)	33 (3)
Other								
Number (Percent)	4 (1)	— (—)	— (—)	12 (*)	2 (*)	4 (1)	2 (*)	7 (*)
Age								
Under 2								
Number (Percent)	44 (9)	242 (15)	53 (10)	175 (8)	458 (38)	145 (30)	167 (10)	186 (14)
2–5								
Number (Percent)	124 (2)	418 (26)	127 (24)	592 (28)	510 (43)	183 (38)	395 (23)	277 (21)
6–11								
Number (Percent)	154 (32)	507 (32)	172 (32)	840 (39)	221 (18)	143 (29)	661 (39)	463 (36)
12 and over								
Number (Percent)	156 (33)	420 (27)	183 (34)	529 (25)	10 (1)	14 (3)	475 (28)	372 (29)

Religion								
Catholic								
Number (Percent)	3 (1)	583 (100)	5 (1)	2,093 (98)	56 (4)	478 (99)	390 (23)	162 (13)
Protestant								
Number (Percent)	81 (17)	4 *	530 (99)	43 (2)	1,136 (95)	7 (1)	1,299 (76)	1,132 (87)
Jewish								
Number (Percent)	394 (82)	— (—)	— (—)	— (—)	7 (1)	— (—)	9 (1)	4 (*)
Sex (Foster boarding home and other[c])								
Male								
Number (Percent)	262 (55)	1,017 (53)	360 (54)	1,092 (51)	680 (57)	249 (51)	896 (52)	627 (48)
Female								
Number (Percent)	216 (45)	911 (47)	309 (46)	1,070 (49)	519 (43)	236 (49)	833 (48)	671 (52)

*Percentages were too small for meaningful calculations.

[a]Latest cost figures for agencies one through six are for foster boarding-home children only and derive from the annual reports of the New York State Department of Social Services for the year ending June 30, 1971. Cost figures were supplied by the Bureau of Child Welfare of the New York City Department of Social Services for agencies seven and eight.

[b]Population figures have been compiled from population reports submitted by these foster-care agencies to the Bureau of Child Welfare of the New York City Department of Social Services, Form 284, rev. September 18, 1968 (New York: June 1972).

[c]Due to the unavailability of data, the distribution by sex is based on the total agency case load—that is, children in all types of placement settings including institutions, group homes, and family homes.

Medical services constituted 80 percent of these expenditures, mental health constituted 16 percent, and dental was 4 percent. Slightly more than half of these costs could be accounted for by in-house services.

Agency Three. This agency, under Protestant auspices, served 535 foster boarding-home children. The case load was almost exclusively Protestant (99 percent) and black (93 percent); only 1 percent were Catholic and 7 percent were white. The medical organization featured a central facility, staffed by one pediatric consultant, one full-time registered nurse, and one clerk. In-house services were limited without regular clinics scheduled. Mental-health care was rendered by one psychiatric consultant, one staff psychiatrist, and two staff psychologists, with outside referrals made as needed. There was no central dental staff. Per capita health costs for this agency totaled $237 per child; about half of this reflects medical services, 36 percent is for mental health, and 14 percent is for dental services.

Agency Four. Under Catholic auspices, this agency operates the largest voluntary foster boarding-home program in New York City. Its case load, at the time of sample selection, consisted of 2,136 children who were predominantly Catholic (98 percent), about 50 percent were white, 22 percent were black, and 27 percent were Puerto Rican. Medical services reportedly were delivered through facilities located in Brooklyn, Queens, and suburban (Nassau and Suffolk) counties, with clinics open approximately seventy-nine hours per week. Staffing these clinics were nine part-time pediatricians, a full-time medical director, seven nurses, and three secretaries. Mental-health professionals included one psychiatrist and five psychologists, all on a part-time basis, and dentists served at one facility, also on a part-time basis. For all other care, outside referrals were made. With regard to costs, the average per capita figure for fiscal year 1970–1971 was $181. Medical services accounted for almost three-fourths of these expenditures, with mental health making up 18 percent and dental, 11 percent.

Agency Five. At the time the sample was drawn, this Protestant agency had 1,199 foster boarding-home children under its jurisdiction. The case load was primarily black (94 percent) and Protestant (95 percent). Only 4 percent were white and 2 percent were Puerto Rican. The medical program featured a medical director available six hours per week and a staff pediatrician available two hours per week, with services coordinated by a full-time registered nurse and two full-time clerical assistants. The agency retained a consulting psychiatrist and a part-time certified psychologist for the provision of in-house mental-health services. Community resources also were utilized. No agency dental staff existed; thus, outside referrals were made for such care. The per capita cost expended in fiscal year 1970–1971 averaged $137 per child. Slightly less than three-fourths of these expenditures represented medical services, one-fifth were for mental health, and 9 percent were for dental.

Agency Six. Four hundred eighty-five children were under the aegis of this facility as of July 1972. The case load was almost exclusively Catholic (99 percent), with Puerto Ricans and whites equally represented (just under 40 percent). Only 22 percent were black. No agency medical or dental facility existed; thus, all such needs were met by outside referrals, coordinated by one medical secretary. To provide centralized mental-health services, the agency retained two part-time psychiatrists and one full-time psychologist. Per capita costs amounted to $119. Mental-health services accounted for 50 percent of these monies; medical, about 40 percent; and dental, 13 percent.

These descriptions reveal the wide variability of the sample at both the intrafacility and interfacility level, along several dimensions, including:

Numbers of foster boarding-home children served, which ranged from 478 to 2,136 per agency;

Centralization versus decentralization of health care, with some agencies offering services on an almost exclusively in-house basis and others making maximal use of community resources for the provision of care;

Per capita Medicaid costs, which ranged from $119 at one agency to $733 at another;

Ethnic and religious composition of the populations served, which varied from predominantly white and Jewish at one agency to exclusively black and Protestant at another to principally Puerto Rican and Catholic at a third.

In addition to the voluntary facilities, two municipal agencies, as previously mentioned, were given a prior inclusion in the sample. Both these facilities serve similar numbers of children (1,698 at agency seven and 1,298 at agency eight) who are predominantly black (81 percent at agency seven and 89 percent at agency eight) and Protestant (76 percent at agency seven and 87 percent at agency eight), and both emphasize decentralized medical services and reported similar per capita expenditures of $83, an amount significantly lower than that expended by the voluntary agencies.

Selection of Sample of Children

Having chosen the agencies, the next stage called for the selection of eligible sample children. Based on cost, logistical, and statistical considerations, it was determined that approximately eighty children per agency would be required for examination and testing.

The universe of children to be sampled was defined as consisting of all New York City public charges who were:

Residing in foster-family homes (that is, those foster children not confined to an institution, residential treatment center, or group home);

In care as of July 1, 1972;

Between the ages of one and fifteen years, inclusive;

Residing in households located within the geographic bounds of the survey (which were the five boroughs of New York City and the westernmost portion of Nassau County, a suburb of New York City).

The determination as to the appropriate status with respect to these conditions was done in several stages. The first involved securing each agency's roster of children in care. Eash list identified the names and ages of children in care as of July 1, 1972. Second, the agencies' rosters of children in care on July 1, 1972, were used as the base from which 130 names were drawn. These names were classified into four equal strata by sex and age group (under six and six and over). It had been anticipated that 130 names would be enough to net a total sample of 80 children to be examined in each agency. However, it soon became apparent that this was not a correct expectation, and a second sample of 130 names was drawn and stratified for each agency.

The agencies' case loads were remarkably mobile. By the time the data-collection phase of the study began in March 1973, an additional 164 children were not available for the examination. Many of the primary-sample children had left foster care, and others had moved to families living beyond the geographic limits of the study area. Some families failed to respond to the invitation to participate in the study; other families refused to participate. In addition, on the day children were scheduled for examination, many were reported to be ill, some had run away from home, and a number became upset at the prospect of the examination.

As is evident, the approach described here, which was dictated by cost and logistical considerations, featured disproportionate sampling within each agency.

Sample Representativeness

The sampling process yielded 1,257 names and ultimately resulted in 1,093 subjects—that is, 425 children who were not examined but for whom historical health and demographic information was available and 668 children for whom a complete set of socioethnic, record-review, and clinical-examination data was collected. These sample cases were classified into eligible cases and ineligible cases.

Of the original pool of 1,257 names selected, 795 met the study's eligibility criteria for participation in the clinical examinations. In all, 84 percent received such evaluations. Among those not examined, the primary reason for nonparticipation (78 out of 127 nonparticipants, or 61 percent) was the refusal of the foster mother to cooperate; other reasons, which were numerically insignificant, included factors such as the child's being away or ill, transportation problems, and a range of miscellaneous reasons. These patterns did not vary significantly across the agencies.

Of the 462 children (42 percent) who did not meet eligibility criteria for inclusion in the project, 21 percent were not within the study's age range, 19 percent could not be contacted, 12 percent were in the process of being removed from foster care, 10 percent lived outside the survey areas, and 3 percent were declared ineligible by the agencies for health-related reasons. Thus, noneligibility was in part a function of population mobility and turnover as these children returned to their own families or were adopted. These factors were distributed evenly across the agencies; others, however, like agency refusal for health reasons, were clustered at particular facilities and appear to reflect certain medical policies in those agencies. For this latter category, however, the numbers involved were too small to permit conclusions on a statistical basis.

Overall, it appears that sample erosion due to unavailability of one kind or another was distributed evenly across the agencies and does not affect the representation of any one facility. However, the loss of 42 percent of the original sample selected within a relatively short period of time is an important confounding variable and a factor of which studies of this type of population must take note.

The extent of potential bias resulting from the 425 nonexamined cases was ascertained for five key variables on which comparable data were available for both the nonevaluated and the evaluated children. These variables were sex, age, ethnicity, chronic medical problem at entry, and admission health status. Such comparisons, while not conclusive, may suggest the extent to which the sample examined deviates from the total population along parameters related to health needs.

From the data in table 2–3, it is evident that there is no difference in the sex ratio of children examined and not examined.

The sample evaluated is overrepresented by two-to-five-year olds and underrepresented by those twelve years and older, but in the largest single category, the six-to-eleven-year age group (which is also the median class), the proportions of children in the examined, not examined, and total sample group are identical (37 percent). Since the overall distributions for

Table 2-3
Sex, Age, Ethnic Group, Admission Health Status, and Chronic Medical
Conditions of Children Examined and Not Examined

Characteristic	Total Number	Total Percent	Children Examined Number	Children Examined Percent	Children Not Examined Number	Children Not Examined Percent
Total	1,093	100	668	100	425	100
Sex						
Male	534	49	330	49	204	48
Female	559	51	338	51	221	52
Age						
Under 2 years	55	5	38	6	17	4
2-5 years	392	36	269	40	123	29
6-11 years	405	37	248	37	157	37
12 years or over	241	22	113	17	128	30
Ethnic Group						
White	227	21	119	18	108	26
Black and other	623	57	430	64	193	45
Puerto Rican	171	16	119	18	52	12
No information	72	6	—	—	72	17
Admission Health Status						
Abnormal	418	38	261	39	157	37
Normal	509	47	312	47	197	46
No information	166	15	95	14	71	17
Chronic Medical Condition						
Had condition	303	28	196	29	107	25
No condition	347	32	209	31	138	33
No information	443	40	263	39	180	42

these groups are quite close, no distorting effects in findings due to age need
be anticipated.

Among those examined, white children are underrepresented and black
children are overrepresented. Except for the latter group, however, the differences are not very large, and these may be disregarded for two reasons.
First, the chi-square test is notably oversensitive to small percentage differences when the numbers are comparatively large, and second, the data
reported in chapter 5 indicate no pronounced or meaningful differences in
health levels between the various ethnic groups. The minor discrepancies
observed, then, do not appear to be of practical importance for this study.

The data in table 2-3 reveal a close similarity between the examined and
not examined group with respect to chronic medical problems at the time
of admission.

Entry Health Status of Children Seen and Not Seen

Medical records were inspected for indications of admission health status as recorded by agency examining physicians. The proportions of children showing some abnormality are indicated in table 2–3.

Among the children examined for whom information was available, about two-fifths were reported to have had some abnormality at the time of admission. The levels for the total group and the not-evaluated group were 38 percent and 37 percent respectively, a nonsignificant difference.

The foregoing analyses of sample representativeness may be summarized as follows:

Criteria		*Significant Differences*
One	Sex	no
Two	Age	yes
Three	Ethnic Group	yes
Four	Health Status at Entry	no
Five	Chronic Medical Condition at Admission	no

Thus, the effect of nonexamination losses appears negligible as far as sex, chronic medical problems, and entry health status are concerned. The discrepancies observed for age and ethnicity, though statistically significant, are marginal, and one may speculate reasonably that the impact of these differences is slight. The general pattern, then, for the characteristics examined suggests that the children evaluated closely approximate the known characteristics of the children not evaluated.

Data Limitations

The effectiveness of any attempt to obtain valid measurements of health and medical care is tempered by problems attendant upon the particular approach used. Despite the fact that many measures were taken throughout this study to ensure that the findings were arrived at in a standardized manner, it may be assumed that some amount of the variability in the results will be due not to real differences in the study groups but to factors such as bias introduced by nonsampled cases (child moved outside survey area, child removed from foster home, foster family could not be contacted/refused to cooperate); examiner and reviewer bias; and agency differentials in administrative policies, record-keeping practices, and case-load characteristics.

In the following chapters, we describe the extent to which particular data may be affected by such measurement error. Of course, one must always be cautious about generalizing the findings of this one city study to the country as a whole. Mindful of these factors, however, our conclusions rest on both limitations and strengths of the study design.

Notes

1. *Bulletin of the New York Academy of Medicine* 44 (February 1968); and Avedis Donabedian, "Evaluating the Quality of Medical Care," *Milbank Memorial Fund Quarterly* 44 (July 1966).

2. Avedis Donabedian, *A Guide to Medical Care Administration, Volume II: Medical Care Appraisal—Quality and Utilization* (New York: American Public Health Association, 1969).

3. K.F. Clute, *The General Practitioner: A Study of Medical Education and Practice in Ontario and Nova Scotia* (Toronto: University of Toronto Press, 1963); and Thomas F. Lyons and Beverly C. Payne, "The Relationship of Physicians' Medical Recording Performance to Their Medical Care Performance," *Medical Care* 12 (August 1974).

4. Hilda H. Kroeger, et al., "The Office Practice of Internists: The Feasibility of Evaluating Quality of Care," *Journal of the American Medical Association* 193 (August 2, 1965); and J. Frederick Eagle, "Quality of Medical Care," *Journal of Pediatrics* 63 (December 1963).

5. *The Reference Manual: Titmas Vision Tester,* revised ed. (Titmas Optical Company, Inc., October 1971).

6. H. Klein et al., "Studies on Dental Caries: Dental Status and Dental Needs of Elementary School Children," *Public Health Reports* 53 (1938):751–765.

7. J.C. Greene, and J.R. Vermillion, "The Simplified Oral Hygiene Index," *Journal of the American Dental Association* 68 (1964):7–13.

8. W.K. Frankenburg, and J.B. Dodds, "The Denver Developmental Screening Test," *Journal of Pediatrics* 71 (August 1967):181–191.

9. W.K. Frankenburg, and J.B. Dodds, *The Denver Developmental Screening Test Manual,* 1968.

10. National Center for Health Statistics, "Evaluation of Psychological Measures Used in the Health Examination of Children Ages 6–11," *Vital and Health Statistics,* Public Health Service pub. no. 1000, series 2, no. 15.

11. D.B. Harris, *Children's Drawings as Measures of Intellectual Maturity* (New York: Harcourt, Brace & World, 1963); and Frankenburg and Dodds, *The Denver Development Screening Test Manual.*

12. Lloyd M. Dunn, Ph.D., *Expanded Manual for the Peabody Picture Test* (Circle Pines, Minn.: American Guidance Service, Inc).

13. Thomas S. Langner et al., "Psychiatric Impairment in Welfare and Non-Welfare Children," *Welfare in Review* 7 (1969):10–21; and Langner et al., "Children of the City: Affluence, Poverty, Mental Health," in *Psychological Factors in Poverty,* ed. Vernon L. Allen (Chicago: Markham Publishing Company, 1970), pp. 185–209.

14. New York City Department of Social Services, "Summary Analysis of Monthly Population Reports Submitted by Foster Care Agencies," mimeographed (New York, June 30, 1972). Religious and ethnic-group designations are as per individual agency definition.

3

Background Characteristics of the Children and Their Families

This chapter examines the biosocial characteristics of the children and their families—specifically, age, sex, ethnicity, and religion; describes family situations and structures; and explores the circumstances surrounding the children's entry into foster care and their histories. In addition, the chapter presents these sociodemographic profiles for the sample children in each study agency. Two cautionary comments are in order. First, the varying availability of background information and, second, the unevenness of agency record-keeping practices, particularly with respect to health data, make interagency comparisons for some variables merely suggestive, not conclusive. Keeping in mind these limitations, however, the detailed and focused picture presented here provides a rough framework for viewing and evaluating the health data developed in later chapters.

The Children

For analytic purposes, the study population was selected in such a way so as to secure a fairly uniform distribution of boys and girls and of children (under age six years) and youths (six to fifteen years), in recognition of the fact that in many areas of child assessment—physical growth, developmental levels, and mental abilities—important sex-and-age-linked differences are reported. Consequently, the data in table 3-1 show that about half of the children were girls (51 percent) and half boys (49 percent). Similarly, the under-six and over-six age groups have roughly equal representation in the sample (46 percent and 54 percent, respectively); the median age falls in the six-to-eleven-year age group. With respect to ethnicity, almost two-thirds of the sample (64 percent) were black or other races, with white and Puerto Rican children each comprising 18 percent of the total group.

Information on religious affiliation was not available for 67.8 percent of the study group, and these data should be viewed with caution. To the extent known, however, Protestants constitute 48 percent of the sample; Catholics, 46 percent; and Jewish, 5 percent.

Table 3-1
Sex and Ethnic Group of Study Children, by Age Group

| Age Group | Total | | Sex | | | | Ethnic Group | | | | | |
| | | | Male | | Female | | White | | Black and Other | | Puerto Rican | |
	Number	Percent	Number	Percent	Number	Percent	Number	Percent	Number	Percent	Number	Percent
Total	668	100	330	100	338	100	119	100	430	100	119	100
Under 2 years	38	6	19	6	19	6	7	6	25	6	6	5
2-5 years	269	40	134	41	135	40	39	33	174	40	56	47
6-11 years	248	37	129	39	119	35	50	42	155	36	43	36
12 years or over	113	17	48	14	65	19	23	19	76	18	14	12

Sex by Age

There is almost no difference in the overall distribution of boys and girls in the study group, with the median ages for both sexes falling within the six-to-eleven-year category. As table 3–2 indicates, though, the proportion of girls slightly exceeds the proportion of boys in the twelve-year-and-over age category, and conversely, boys exceed girls in the six-to-eleven-year age category by a few percentage points. The observed differences are too small, however, to be meaningful.

Ethnicity by Age

When ethnicity and age are considered together, we note only minor differences within the study group (see table 3–1). Puerto Rican children, with a median age in the two-to-five-year category, were slightly though not significantly younger than black and white children, for whom the median age was within the six-to-eleven-year group. Proportionately, 47 percent of the Puerto Rican children were between two and five years, as contrasted with 40 percent of the blacks and 33 percent of the whites. Somewhat fewer Puerto Rican than black and white children fell within the twelve-year-and-over age category (12 percent as contrasted with 18 percent and 19 percent, respectively), but these differences were not statistically significant.

With regard to interagency differences, there was little variation with respect to either the sex distribution or the proportion of children in the under- or over-six-year classes (table 3–2). Median ages for the different facilities were close to the median for the whole sample, except in agencies two and six, where children were somewhat younger than elsewhere, and the median age is between two and five years compared with six to eleven for all other facilities. This statistic is not, however, overly sensitive to distributions of dissimilar shapes, and the age distributions did differ within specific class intervals and in their overall contours. These differences were most pronounced at the extremes. Thus, the proportion of infants under two years of age ranged from zero at one agency to 13 percent at another, while for youths (twelve and over) the percentages varied from a low of 8 percent to a high of 28 percent. Despite these deviations at the extremes, the data indicate that the great majority of children (77 percent) were in the two central age groups (two through five years and six through eleven years), with proportions within the agencies ranging from 64 percent to 90 percent.

It appears, then, that these facilities tend to draw upon somewhat differing age groups, and in fact, available citywide data confirm this impression.[1] To be sure, the varying nature of administrative and entry policies among these agencies contributes in part to these observed differences.

Table 3-2
Percentage Distribution of Age, Sex, and Ethnic Group of Study Children, by Agency

Characteristic	Total Classified (n = 668)	Agency							
		One (n = 78)	Two (n = 83)	Three (n = 86)	Four (n = 77)	Five (n = 91)	Six (n = 85)	Seven (n = 81)	Eight (n = 87)
Total	100	100	100	100	100	100	100	100	100
Age									
Under 2 years	6	13	11	8	—	4	2	6	1
2-5 years	40	23	40	40	45	42	49	40	43
6-11 years	37	41	41	24	46	41	32	36	38
12 years or over	17	23	8	28	9	13	17	18	18
Sex									
Male	49	54	49	50	47	49	48	48	49
Female	51	46	51	50	53	51	52	52	51
Ethnic group									
White	18	59	17	1	28	5	20	6	2
Black and other	64	41	25	99	32	93	42	79	96
Puerto Rican	18	—	58	—	30	2	38	15	2

Chi square for age = 25.542, $p < .01$.
Chi square for sex is not significant.
Chi square for ethnic group = 580.31, $p < .001$.

The sampled agencies also show differences with respect to ethnicity, with some serving predominantly black children (agencies three, five, seven, and eight), others serving biracial children, and a few serving almost equal proportions of white, black, and Puerto Rican children (table 3-5). For the agencies that are composed principally of blacks and other races, the proportions range from 79 percent at agency seven to 99 percent at agency three. The biracial facilities, agencies one and two, have the following distributions respectively: 59 percent white, 41 percent black and other races; 58 percent Puerto Rican, 25 percent black and other races, and 17 percent white. In the remaining agencies (four and six), each ethnic group has approximately equal representation. All differences are significant.

A slight rearrangement of the data makes ethnic-group differences across agencies somewhat clearer. Thus, table 3-2 shows the largest proportions of white children clustered in agencies one, four, and six; black children in agencies three, five, and eight; and Puerto Rican children at agencies two, four, and six. Agencies one, four, and six account for 77 percent of the white children; agencies three, five, and eight account for 60 percent of the black children; and agencies two, four, and six account for 86 percent of the Puerto Rican children. Puerto Rican clientele are most heavily concentrated in their three principal agencies, white are next, and blacks are somewhat more widely scattered. In general, then, agencies appear to be stratified by ethnic group. The implications of these variations with respect to health differentials are explored later.

The Natural Families

Ethnic-Group and Religious Affiliation

More than three-fifths of the children had black or interracial mothers, over one-fifth had white mothers, and nearly one-fifth had Puerto Rican mothers. The racial profile of the fathers, to the extent known, roughly parallels the figures for the mothers. Comparison with data reported for the children reveals almost identical distributions, as might be expected, suggesting a high level of ethnic homogeneity.

Fifty percent of the mothers were Protestant, 40 percent were Catholic, and 9 percent were Jewish (table 3-3). Data on religious affiliation of the natural father, as for the sample of the children, were quite incomplete. With this caveat in mind, however, it was noted that the distributions for the fathers, the children, and the mothers are in close agreement, a finding suggestive of a high degree of familial demographic homogeneity.

Concerning religious affiliation, the profile for the mothers (92 percent reported) indicates significant differences across the agencies (see table 3-3)

Table 3–3
Percentage Distribution of Religion of Natural Mothers, by Agency

Religion	Total Classified (n = 615)	Agency							
		One (n = 75)	Two (n = 81)	Three (n = 74)	Four (n = 75)	Five (n = 86)	Six (n = 70)	Seven (n = 72)	Eight (n = 82)
Total	100	100	100	100	100	100	100	100	100
Protestant	50	33	1	96	8	93	6	67	89
Catholic	40	3	99	4	89	5	89	32	10
Jewish	9	64	—	—	1	2	1	1	1
Other	1	—	—	—	2	—	4	—	—
Number unknown	53	3	2	12	2	5	15	9	5

and corresponds with the religious auspices under which the voluntary facilities operate (see chapter 2) and the known religious profile of the city agencies. Thus, the natural mothers were principally Jewish at agency one; Catholic at agencies two, four, and six; and Protestant at agencies three, five, seven, and eight. Since the religious affiliations of husbands and wives and parents and children are highly correlated, the maternal profile suggests corresponding results for the children and their fathers.

Education

Data on educational level were available for 418 mothers (63 percent of the sample) but for only 154 fathers (23 percent). Nineteen percent of the mothers for whom data were available were high school graduates, and 29 percent had had only a grammar school education or less (table 3–4). About one in twenty (5 percent) had had some college, and 2 percent were reported to be college graduates. The educational profile of the fathers, to the extent known, roughly parallels that of the mothers.

Across the agencies, the extent to which information on education was available ranged from 44 percent (agency seven) to 79 percent (agency five), an unevenness that limits the reliability of the data. With these cautions in mind, it can be noted that educational levels appear to vary somewhat from one agency to another. Thus, while the median educational level for the total sample group and for each facility except one (agency five, where the median fell in the high-school-graduate educational class) fell within the some-high-school educational category, the proportion of mothers who were not high school graduates varied from 45 percent to 94 percent across the agencies. Further, those who had completed high school (19 percent), had had some college (5 percent), or were college graduates (2 percent) were concentrated primarily in four facilities (one, two, five, and six). The high degree of missing information makes these findings merely suggestive, however, and not indicative of meaningful differences among these agencies.

Family Structure

Social data indicate that level of family impairment, a variable often associated with pathologies of various kinds, may be roughly scaled as intact (both parents in household), partially intact (one parent missing), and impaired (that is, the condition in which a once-complete nuclear family has been parcelled out among various relatives and casual acquaintances).

For the children in this study, only 20 percent reportedly were living in intact families in the year prior to foster placement, 36 percent were with one parent, and 22 percent were with relatives, friends, or others (see table

Table 3-4
Percentage Distribution of Formal Education of Natural Mothers, by Agency

Education Completed	Total Classified (n = 418)	One (n = 59)	Two (n = 46)	Three (n = 52)	Four (n = 46)	Five (n = 72)	Six (n = 49)	Seven (n = 36)	Eight (n = 58)
						Agency			
Total	100	100	100	100	100	100	100	100	100
Grammar school or less	29	20	37	44	46	6	39	33	24
Some high school	45	46	35	48	48	39	49	45	52
High school graduate	19	19	20	6	6	43	4	22	22
College or beyond	7	15	8	2	—	12	8	—	2
Number unknown	250	19	37	34	31	19	36	45	29

Note: As recorded in agency social records.

Table 3–5
Household Composition of Natural Families, by Ethnic Group

			Ethnic Group					
	Total		White		Black and Other		Puerto Rican	
Household Composition	Number	Percent	Number	Percent	Number	Percent	Number	Percent
Total	668	100	119	100	430	100	119	100
Intact	131	20	51	43	51	12	29	24
Partially intact	239	36	43	36	140	33	56	47
Impaired	148	22	18	15	105	24	25	21
Unknown	150	22	7	6	134	31	9	8

5). For 20 percent of the cases the family structure was unknown. While it is difficult to make precise comparisons of percentages from different sources, the proportion of known incomplete families here is apparently consistent with that reported in other contemporary surveys (see chapter 5).

When ethnicity and family structure are correlated, we find that significantly fewer black than white children lived with both parents (12 percent and 43 percent, respectively), while the Puerto Rican families were intermediate in this respect (24 percent). Correspondingly fewer white children derive from the more-impaired or scattered households: 21 percent were classified as impaired and unknown, compared with 55 percent of the black and 29 percent of the Puerto Rican children. These data suggest that among households generating a foster-care population, white family structure is moderately intact, black composition may be relatively impaired, and that of Puerto Ricans is somewhat intermediate between the two groups.

In terms of interagency data, the largest single category for all but one agency (agency three) was the single-parent household. This category accounted for 46 percent of the study group and ranged from a low of 21 percent to a high of 63 percent across agencies (see table 3–6).

Family Income

Data on source of income were unavailable for 30 percent of the study group. Despite this, the overall picture reveals the marginal level at which many of these families lived. For 63 percent of the remaining households, public assistance was the main source of income, 27 percent earned salaries, and another 10 percent relied upon pensions or social-security payments (table 3–6).

Table 3–6
Percentage Distribution of Household Composition and Source of Income of Natural Parents, by Agency

Natural-Family Variable	Total Classified	Agency							
		One	Two	Three	Four	Five	Six	Seven	Eight
Total	100	100	100	100	100	100	100	100	100
	(n = 518)	(n = 75)	(n = 79)	(n = 19)	(n = 68)	(n = 55)	(n = 78)	(n = 69)	(n = 75)
Household composition									
Intact	25	36	25	37	35	5	38	12	16
Partially intact	46	45	43	21	41	40	55	39	63
Impaired	11	—[a]	8	—[a]	6	31	3	33	7
Other	18	19	24	42	18	24	4	16	14
Number unknown	150	3	4	67	9	36	7	12	12
Main source of income	(n = 468)	(n = 61)	(n = 57)	(n = 50)	(n = 56)	(n = 50)	(n = 68)	(n = 56)	(n = 70)
Salary	27	38	14	20	25	46	28	25	23
Public assistance	63	51	72	56	70	44	69	64	73
All other sources	10	11	14	24	5	10	3	11	4
Number unknown	200	17	26	36	21	41	17	25	17

[a]Insufficient to percentage.

Table 3–7
Public-Assistance Status of Natural Families, by Ethnic Group

Public Assistance Status	Total		White		Black and Other		Puerto Rican	
	Number	Percent	Number	Percent	Number	Percent	Number	Percent
Total	668	100	119	100	430	100	119	100
Yes	295	44	39	33	183	43	73	61
No	173	26	51	43	107	25	15	13
Unknown	200	30	29	24	140	32	31	26

Across the agencies these proportions on public assistance ranged from slightly less than half (44 percent) in agency five to almost three-quarters (73 percent) in agency eight. Although the large number of cases on which information was not obtained makes conclusions somewhat uncertain, these data further confirm that the children, agency by agency, derive from families of marginal economic circumstances.

Using the percentages of the total sample including the unknowns, we observe striking differences by ethnic group (table 3–7). Significantly more Puerto Rican than white families were supported by public assistance (61 percent versus 33 percent), with black households (43 percent) intermediate in this respect. The proportion of unknown is evenly distributed among the three ethnic groups.

For the total sample, though the socioeconomic data described here are somewhat incomplete, the picture that emerges conforms to expectations. For the most part, the families from which these foster children are derived subsist on low incomes, many below the poverty level; are disproportionately black and Puerto Rican; are below average in years of schooling completed; and show a high level of family impairment.

Placement Histories

The circumstances surrounding a child's separation from his home are typically complex and diverse, suggestive of a multiplicity of factors acting upon the families. For the current study, a primary reason for placement was identified as the most critical factor in the decision to place the child. While this is useful for analytic purposes, it should be noted that significant secondary and tertiary causes contribute to every placement.

Four major reasons for placement have been identified in table 3–8:

Table 3-8
Percentage Distribution of Reason for Placement of Study Children, by Ethnic Group and Agency

Reason for Placement	Ethnic Group	Total Classified[a] (n = 626)	One (n = 76)	Two (n = 82)	Three (n = 81)	Four (n = 73)	Five (n = 72)	Six (n = 84)	Seven (n = 77)
Total		100	100	100	100	100	100	100	100
Physical illness or incapacity of child-caring person	All	27	24	39	2	32	36	29	22
	White	23	16	29	—	31	b	29	b
	Nonwhite[c]	28	35	41	3	32	37	28	22
Mental illness of mother or child-caring person	All	23	41	20	46	15	6	20	11
	White	38	56	29	b	21	b	35	b
	Nonwhite[c]	19	19	18	46	11	4	16	11
Abandonment, desertion and other family dysfunction	All	25	18	12	34	27	51	18	31
	White	19	18	14	b	10	b	18	b
	Nonwhite[c]	27	19	12	33	39	51	18	30
Severe neglect or abuse	All	24	17	28	17	26	7	31	36
	White	19	11	21	—	38	—	12	b
	Nonwhite[c]	25	26	29	18	18	7	36	37

Note: Total n = 626 for all eight agencies. Data not indicated for agency eight with n = 81.
[a]Information was unavailable for 6 percent of study group.
[b]Numbers too small for meaningful percentaging.
[c]Includes Puerto Ricans.

physical illness or incapacity of the mother or child-caring person (27 percent); mental illness of the mother or child-caring person, identified because of hospitalization or professional diagnosis (23 percent); abandonment, desertion, or other types of family dysfunction (25 percent); and severe neglect or abuse of the child (24 percent). Problems of the children accounted for less than 1 percent of the entry reasons.

Table 3–8 shows some differences between white and other ethnic groups with respect to major reasons for placement. In cases where information is available, white children were more frequently placed because of mental illness of the mother (38 percent compared with 19 percent of the nonwhite children). Among nonwhites, the principal reason for placement was the physical illness or incapacity of the child-caring person (28 percent), closely followed by abandonment and desertion (27 percent for nonwhites and 19 percent for whites). Similarly, severe neglect or abuse of the child accounted for 25 percent of nonwhite compared with 19 percent of white placements.

On an interagency level, reason for placement differs sharply and significantly in marked contrast to the relatively even distribution across the total sample, where each accounts for close to one-fourth of the cases. Thus, agencies one (41 percent) and three (46 percent) show a high rate of placements due to mental illness of the mother, whereas agencies five (6 percent) and seven (11 percent) exhibit an underrepresentation in this category. Physical illness as a factor contributing to entry occurs in above-average levels at agencies two (39 percent) and five (36 percent) and in below-average levels in agency three (2 percent). Severe neglect and abuse is an important placement category at agencies six (31 percent) and seven (36 percent), and the category of abandonment and desertion accounts for a disproportionate percentage of agency five (51 percent) placements. All differences are statistically significant.

Thus, the agencies present somewhat different profiles of the types of problems that precipitate the need for substitute care among their clientele. Closer examination of these data by ethnic group within each agency shows, though, that interagency differentials are less striking than interethnic variations. As may be seen in table 3–19, white:nonwhite ratios among placement categories remain relatively constant across the study facilities, almost without exception, and agency fluctuations appear to be related in large part to the differing ethnic characteristics of the children comprising their case loads.

Source of Referral

The mode of entry into foster care further reflects the nature and level of family dysfunction. The intervention of the court or police presumably suggests the severest level of family breakdown.

Involuntary or enforced separations account for the majority of place-ments among these children. The data in table 3–9 indicate that 20 percent of the study children for whom information is given were placed as a result of the intervention of the court or the police, that a somewhat higher pro-portion (24 percent) were placed voluntarily by their relatives, and that more than half (54 percent) entered care through the involvement of either a public-welfare agency, social worker, or hospital facility.

The nature of the separation experience, whether voluntary (that is, parent or friend initiated) or involuntary (that is, court or Bureau of Child Welfare initiated), showed considerable agency variation, as might be ex-pected from the differing subpopulations and administrative policies of the eight participating facilities. While more than half (54 percent) of the children in the study entered care under the aegis of the New York City Bureau of Child Welfare, social workers, or hospitals, the proportions across the agencies ranged from a low of 31 percent to a high of 100 percent.

Similar differences were observed for the two other major referral sources. Voluntary placements, for example, constituted 24 percent of total study referral sources but varied by facility, from zero to 41 percent, with high percentages at agencies one, six, and seven. Involuntary or enforced separations, without exception, were the predominant mode of entry for children within each agency.

We presume that this pattern of separation, involving the intervention of the court or public agency, is suggestive of more-serious family difficul-ties or more-precipitous crisis situations than one might expect from a more-voluntaristic mode of entry.

Age at Time of Admission

These children first came into foster care at fairly young ages. Over four-fifths (83 percent) were placed as preschoolers, about five in every eight children (62 percent) entered care under two years of age, and 21 percent entered between two and six years (table 3–10).

As with the preceding background variables, agencies varied with respect to the age at which their clientele were placed. Whereas the median entry age for the total sample falls between three months and two years of age, specific facilities exhibited different distributions. Agencies one, six, and seven appear to admit children at somewhat older age levels, and agen-cies two and five show younger entry ages for their clientele. Since the latter two agencies are, respectively, a foundling hospital and an adoptive (as well as foster-care) agency, their earlier placements are not unexpected.

When ethnicity and age at admission are considered together, we find significant differences across the three categories of racial identification—

Table 3-9
Percentage Distribution of Source of Referral of Study Children, by Agency

Source of Referral	Total Classified (n = 625)	Agency							
		One (n = 76)	Two (n = 82)	Three (n = 85)	Four (n = 73)	Five (n = 70)	Six (n = 84)	Seven (n = 76)	Eight (n = 79)
Total	100	100	100	100	100	100	100	100	100
Bureau of Child Welfare, social worker, hospital	54	33	61	100	45	79	31	31	51
Police, Court	20	28	27	—	22	4	24	31	23
Parents, relatives, friend	24	38	12	—	29	11	41	37	26
Other	2	1	—	—	4	6	4	1	—
Number unknown	43	2	1	1	4	21	1	5	8

Chi square = 71.05, $p < .001$.

Table 3–10
Percentage Distribution of Age at Placement of Study Children, by Agency

Age at Placement	Total Classified (n = 650)	Agency							
		One (n = 78)	Two (n = 83)	Three (n = 85)	Four (n = 69)	Five (n = 88)	Six (n = 85)	Seven (n = 78)	Eight (n = 84)
Total	100	100	100	100	100	100	100	100	100
Under 3 months	27	18	35	20	33	58	12	13	23
3 months to under 2 years	35	30	52	31	29	39	36	29	35
2 to under 6 years	21	22	12	30	26	2	27	26	21
6 to under 12 years	15	27	1	19	12	1	20	22	19
12 years or over	2	3	—	—	—	—	5	10	2
Number unknown	18	—	—	1	8	3	—	3	3
Median age (months)	14	26	9	3	13	2	28	39	19

Chi square (21 d.f.) = 141.06, $p < .005$.

black children tended to be younger at entry than white or Puerto Rican children. Thus, we see from table 3-11 that far more black (30 percent) than white (18 percent) or Puerto Rican children (20 percent) were admitted to care under three months of age. The median entry ages for the three groups—fifteen, twenty, and eighteen months respectively—similarly reflect these ethnic differentials.

Number and Type of Placement

Once placed in foster homes, these children had a two-in-five chance of experiencing multiple placements. For those for whom data are available, 58 percent had only one placement, 28 percent had two, and 14 percent had three or more placements (table 3-12). Most received care in foster-family homes (83 percent); only 12.5 percent were placed in institutions and group homes; and other settings accounted for 5 percent of the remaining types reported. Although 58 percent of the study group had experienced only one placement since entry, this proportion varied considerably across agencies, from a low of 20 percent (agency two) to a high of 79 percent (agency eight). Multiple placements occurred in disproportionate numbers at agencies two

Table 3-11
Age of Study Children at Time of Admission, by Ethnic Group

				Ethnic Group			
Age at	Total		White		Black and Other		Puerto Rican	
Admission	Number	Percent	Number	Percent	Number	Percent	Number	Percent
Total	668	100	119	100	430	100	119	100
Under 3 months	173	26	21	18	128	30	24	20
3 months to 2 years	230	34	47	39	133	31	50	42
2-6 years	161	24	34	29	101	23	26	22
6-12 years	70	11	14	12	42	10	14	12
12 years and over	16	2	2	2	12	3	2	2
Unknown	18	3	1	1	14	3	3	3
Median age (months)	16		20		15		18	

$p < .05.$

Table 3-12
Percentage Distribution of Number of Placements Since Admission of Study Children, by Agency

Number of Placements	Total Classified (n = 633)	Agency							
		One (n = 78)	Two (n = 82)	Three (n = 76)	Four (n = 71)	Five (n = 87)	Six (n = 83)	Seven (n = 76)	Eight (n = 80)
Total	100	100	100	100	100	100	100	100	100
One	58	63	20	75	37	68	57	69	79
Two	28	27	53	13	38	23	29	20	17
Three	8	8	16	7	10	6	6	8	4
Four or more	6	2	11	5	15	3	8	3	—
Number unknown	35	—	1	10	6	4	2	5	7

Note: Based on data collected from agency social records.

Chi square = 65, $p < .005$.

(80 percent) and four (63 percent). Single placements predominated at agencies three (75 percent), seven (69 percent), and eight (79 percent).

Length of Time in Care

The mean length of time in placement was 4.9 years; the median falls in the four-year category, the mode in the six-years-or-more group (table 3-13).

Analysis of length of stay and age at admission yields a large clustering of cases in the over-six-years-old age category. There appears to be a tendency for these children, once placed, to remain in foster care. On an interagency level, the number of years children had been in care showed major deviations for agencies six and seven, which reported means below the group level of four years, and agency five, which showed a mean above this overall figure. These same agencies differed markedly from the sample average for age at admission (see section on age at admission), with the former facilities admitting children at somewhat older ages and the latter at considerably younger ages. While these data suggest that entry age may be inversely related to age at admission, the pattern is not consistent across all agencies.

In brief, we have presented thus far some aspects of the placement histories of the sample group. For the most part, the children came from relatively disadvantaged lower-income families. Maternal physical and mental illness was the dominant reason for the placement of the child. Most of the children had been separated involuntarily from their parents through the intervention of a court or social agency. The average child was placed as a preschooler, and over 40 percent were placed more than once; more than half had been in care four or more years, and a minority had been in care less than two years. In addition, this presentation of placement data showed statistically significant interagency differences for all variables considered. Since agencies, however, did not deviate consistently from the characteristics of the total sample with respect to each factor examined, it would appear that the case loads they service are drawn from subpopulations having distinctive sociodemographic profiles that tend to become blurred when aggregated.

Health Histories

Familial Health Profiles

The familial health picture is incomplete, making group comparisons rough and statistical testing of questionable value. Nonetheless, with these cau-

Table 3–13
Percentage Distribution of Length of Time in Placement of Study Children, by Agency

Length of Time in Placement	Total Classified (n = 653)	Agency							
		One (n = 78)	Two (n = 83)	Three (n = 85)	Four (n = 69)	Five (n = 88)	Six (n = 85)	Seven (n = 80)	Eight (n = 87)
Total (n = 653)	100	100	100	100	100	100	100	100	100
One year or less (1972–1973) (n = 653)	11	15	4	14	1	9	15	20	—
Two years (n = 117)	18	19	19	19	13	13	12	35	1
Three years (n = 88)	13	17	9	11	19	6	18	15	1
Four years (n = 82)	13	8	19	8	10	5	21	13	1
Five years (n = 69)	11	12	7	7	9	10	23	6	—
Six years or more (before 1968) (n = 225)	34	29	42	41	48	57	11	11	3
Mean number of years in care	4.92	4.56	5.77	5.39	5.43	6.48	3.66	3.09	4.8
Number unknown	15	—	—	1	6	3	—	1	2

Chi square = 114, $p < .005$.

tions in mind, it may be noted that two-fifths of the mothers for whom data were available were reported to have a history of mental illness. Across the agencies, the proportion of mentally ill mothers ranged from a low of one-fifth (20 percent) to a high of three-fifths (63 percent), with mothers in agencies one and three more likely to have mental illness and those in agencies five and eight less likely. Again, however, sketchy data preclude conclusive interpretations.

Information on the physical-health status of the mothers was also incomplete: 20 percent had some problem and 28 percent had no problem, but physical-health data were not available for half the sample. Similarly for the fathers, health profiles were rarely ascertainable.

Though the picture is sketchy, the results are suggestive of a situation in which substantial proportions of study children, agency by agency, derive from families exhibiting relatively high levels of health impairment. These data are consistent with our findings that half of the study children were placed primarily because of physical and mental illness of the parent (see table 3-8). It may be noted further that the unevenness with which the various agencies are aware of familial health levels may be indicative of differential casework and record-keeping policies, practices, and staffing patterns.

Birth Histories

In view of the precipitious nature of many foster-care placements and the instability of the backgrounds from which such children derive, it is not surprising that full information on birth histories was not always available. Though in a strict sense interagency comparisons cannot be made, the fact that low birth weight and birth anomalies are highly correlated with later morbidity makes these data, to the extent reported, worthy of mention. Table 3-14 shows that 18 percent of the study children were reported to be of low birth weight (under 5 lb., 9 oz.), that 41 percent were 5 lb., 9 oz. or more, but that data were unavailable also for 41 percent. While agency variations, to be sure, reflect in part the varying levels of missing information, it is noteworthy that low-birth-weight rates ranged from a low of 9 percent to a high of 29 percent, with agencies one, two, and five showing an overabundance and agencies six and eight an underabundance of such children. These figures are high by comparison with the rates reported for other study groups, which range from 7 percent through 14 percent.[2]

These agency data, to the extent known, are indicative of a high rate of prematurity even when compared with New York City figures.

An attempt to secure further evidence relating to health problems at birth yielded even less-complete data. As may be seen from table 3-15, 16

Table 3–14
Percentage Distribution of Birth Weights of Study Children, by Agency

Birth weights	Study Total (n = 668)	Agency							
		One (n = 78)	Two (n = 83)	Three (n = 86)	Four (n = 77)	Five (n = 91)	Six (n = 85)	Seven (n = 81)	Eight (n = 87)
Total	100	100	100	100	100	100	100	100	100
Low birth weight (under 5 lb., 9 oz.)									
3 lb., 8 oz. or less	4	5	5	—	4	9	—	5	2
3 lb., 9 oz.– 5 lb., 8 oz.	14	16	24	17	8	17	9	10	7
Total low birth weight	18	21	29	17	12	26	9	15	9
Birth weight of 5 lb., 9 oz. and over	41	42	64	42	28	64	24	23	40
Unknown	41	37	7	41	60	10	67	62	51

Note: In New York City low birth weights occurred in 10.1 percent (1965), 9.7 percent (1970), and 9.1 percent (1974). For births to nonwhites these figures are 15.7 percent, 13.9 percent, and 12.9 percent, respectively. (Source: Office of Statistics, New York City Department of Health.)

Table 3–15
Percentage Distribution of Health Conditions Present at Birth of Study Children, by Agency

Condition	Study Total (n = 668)	Agency							
		One (n = 78)	Two (n = 83)	Three (n = 86)	Four (n = 77)	Five (n = 91)	Six (n = 85)	Seven (n = 81)	Eight (n = 87)
Total percentage	100	100	100	100	100	100	100	100	100
No apparent abnormality	34	21	47	49	21	58	13	24	37
Some abnormality									
Drug-withdrawal syndrome	6	9	12	6	1	3	6	5	2
Congenital malformation	5	4	4	2	1	12	7	6	—
Respiratory difficulties	4	5	11	2	—	8	2	1	2
All other conditions	1	1	6	1	—	—	2	—	—
Total abnormalities	16	19	33	11	2	23	17	12	4
Unknown condition	50	60	20	40	77	19	70	64	59

percent of the total sample was reported to have had some health-related problem at the time of birth and 34 percent had no problem, but for half the sample information was unavailable.

Among the conditions identified, the drug-withdrawal syndrome occurred most frequently (6 percent), followed by congenital malformations (5 percent) and respiratory problems (4 percent). Across the agencies, from 2 percent to 33 percent were classified as having had some problem, with agencies one, two, and five again at the high end of the scale and agencies four and eight at the low end. Though the level of missing data makes interfacility comparisons somewhat difficult, the overall picture, even with these sketchy data, shows some consistency. This suggests the possibility that these variations reflect more than simply differences in casework or record-keeping practices.

Health Status at Time of Admission

Admission health status was ascertained by two measures: (1) Normal or abnormal general health status and (2) recommendations for specialty-care referrals (table 3-16). On both these parameters, the eight participating facilities differed significantly. Thus, while abnormal evaluations were reported for 46 percent of the sample group, across the agencies proportions varied from a low of 19 percent to a high of 59 percent, with children at agencies one (59 percent) and two (58 percent) exhibiting the highest percentages of adverse findings and those in agency eight (19 percent) with the lowest. The data for referrals show similar marked variations, with an average of 12 percent referred for care in the entire sample and an agency range of 3 percent to 21 percent. Again, agencies one (21 percent) and two (18 percent) appear high and the low (5 percent) is at agency eight. The degree to which these variations reflect dissimilar subpopulations rather than differential health-assessment practices cannot be answered by these data alone. It is, however, noteworthy that agencies are expected to perform complete physical evaluations at the time of admission and that for 14 percent of these children, primarily representing agencies six, seven, and eight, no such assessment was reported.

Health Histories: 1968-1973

Health levels of study children during the five-year period prior to the beginning of this investigation (with data adjusted for age and length of time in placement) were ascertained through the collection of data from agency records pertaining to abnormalities detected by agency physicians,

Table 3–16
Percentage Distribution of Admission Health Status and Referrals Recommended of Study Children, by Agency

Variable	Total Classified (n = 573)	One (n = 78)	Two (n = 80)	Three (n = 81)	Four (n = 76)	Five (n = 91)	Six (n = 63)	Seven (n = 46)	Eight (n = 58)
						Agencies			
Total	100	100	100	100	100	100	100	100	100
Admission health status[a]									
Abnormal	46	59	58	32	49	55	48	33	19
Normal	53	41	41	68	49	45	49	67	81
Cannot determine	1	—	1	—	2	—	3	—	—
Referrals recommended[b]									
Yes	12	21	18	14	12	3	8	13	5
No	87	79	80	86	87	97	90	83	95
Cannot determine	1	—	2	—	1	—	2	4	—
Number of children with no admission exam recorded	95	—	3	5	1	—	22	35	29

[a]Chi square $p < .01$.
[b]Chi square $p < .01$.
Note: Based on agency physicians' evaluations recorded in agency medical records.

chronic health problems, and hospitalizations, length of stay, and diagnoses.

The level of abnormality detected by physicians during the performance of preventive health examinations shows significant agency variation. Although the average number per agency for the entire group was 0.40 across the agencies, this measure varied sharply from a low of 0.13 (agency eight) to a high of 0.61 (agency one). These differences are significant, but the extent to which they reflect the varying nature of the medical-care processes rather than the needs of the subpopulations served requires further exploration.

The distribution of chronic health problems identified in agency medical records is presented in table 3-17. Mental disorders represented 25 percent of the problems reported, varying from a low of 17 percent (agency three) to a high of 31 percent (agency one).

Among physical disabilities, eye disorders were the leading category, comprising 14 percent of the total, followed by congenital anomalies (11 percent), musculoskeletal and respiratory conditions (each 10 percent), nutritional/metabolic problems (9 percent), and digestive and cardiovascular disorders (each 6 percent). The remaining categories each constituted 5 percent or less of the total.

Although agency by agency the five leading classes of physical disorders constituted the majority of problems reported, these conditions occur in somewhat different relative frequencies. Thus, chronic respiratory disorders were most numerous at agencies four and eight, and nutritional/metabolic problems were most numerous at agency one. While all differences were statistically significant, no consistent pattern emerged. These data alone, then, do not seem to reflect any salient factors that might differentiate the agencies.

Information pertaining to the hospitalization experiences of study children is presented in table 3-18. As may be observed, about one-fourth of the group had one or more hospital episodes during the period 1968-1973. (Data are adjusted for age and length of time in placement.) This measure varied significantly among the agencies, from a low of 10 percent to annual hospitalization rates. Thus, agency two, at the high end of the scale, reported approximately four times as many hospital episodes per year as agency eight, at the low end of the scale. All differences were significant.

Concerning length of stay per episode, the average for the total group was about 22 days, but among the agencies this figure ranged from almost 15 days (agency one) to 35 days (agency three). Examination of the medians reveals a somewhat different pattern, however: 8 days per episode for the entire group, and an agency range of 4.5 (agency one) to 14 days (agency five).

Table 3-17

Percentage Distribution of Chronic Health Problems of Study Children Recorded in Agency Medical Record, by Agency, 1968–1973

Chronic Problems	Total Classified (n = 1,076)	Agency							
		One (n = 244)	Two (n = 193)	Three (n = 161)	Four (n = 165)	Five (n = 122)	Six (n = 109)	Seven (n = 90)	Eight (n = 92)
Total	100	100	100	100	100	100	100	100	100
Mental disorders	25	31	28	17	21	22	23	26	30
Physical disorders									
Eye conditions	14	12	13	14	14	14	17	13	12
Congenital anomalies	11	5	11	9	14	16	14	17	7
Musculosceletal	10	12	12	10	12	12	7	6	4
Respiratory	10	7	7	11	15	4	9	13	17
Nutritional/ metabolic	9	14	5	12	4	9	—	6	9
Digestive	6	4	6	5	6	6	8	3	9
Cardiovascular	6	6	5	4	6	7	4	7	8
Speech conditions	5	5	4	4	5	7	5	3	3
Nervous-system disorders	3	2	4	6	1	1	6	4	1
All other chronic problems	3	2	3	8	2	2	3	2	—

Chi square = 135.701, d.f. = 70, $p < .001$.

Table 3-18
Annual Rate, Percentage Distribution, and Length of Stay of Hospital Episodes, by Agency, 1968–1973

Hospital Episodes	Study Total (n = 668)	Agency							
		One (n = 78)	Two (n = 83)	Three (n = 86)	Four (n = 77)	Five (n = 91)	Six (n = 85)	Seven (n = 81)	Eight (n = 87)
Annual rate per child[a]	0.13	0.16	0.27	0.21	0.06	0.12	0.14	0.06	0.03
WTD SUM	88	12	22	18	5	11	11	5	3
STD DEV	.367	.459	.594	.438	.164	.368	.286	.160	.130
SE MEAN	.014	.052	.065	.047	.019	.039	.031	.018	.014
Percent distribution[b]									
Total	100	100	100	100	100	100	100	100	100
None	76	76	58	66	79	79	76	84	90
One	16	15	26	22	17	12	11	14	9
Two	5	4	10	8	3	7	11	1	1
Three or more	3	5	6	4	1	2	2	1	c
Length of stay per episode in days									
Mean	21.9	14.7	17.4	35.1	19.4	28.4	20.5	17.3	14.8
Median	8	4.5	8	9.5	7	14	13	8	7
WTD SUM	4297	484	1044	1229	136	768	389	173	74
STD DEV	40.545	25.198	29.328	71.570	32.186	38.318	27.756	23.305	19.01
SE MEAN	2.896	4.386	3.786	12.097	12.165	7.374	6.368	7.370	8.50
Mean-median differences	13.9	10.2	9.4	25.6	12.4	14.4	7.5	9.3	7.8

Note: Recorded in Agency Medical Records.
WTD SUM = weighted sum   STD DEV = standard deviation   SE MEAN = standard error of the mean.
[a] F ratio for annual hospitalization rate = 3.160, $p < .10$.
[b] Chi square for number of episodes = 30.334, $p < .001$.
[c] Less than 0.5 percent.

Thus, although there is variability between the agencies, the variation within the agencies is much greater, suggesting that the conditions that cause hospitalizations vary considerably with regard to type and severity. This can be evidenced by further inspection of table 3-18 that also shows the differences between the mean and median length of stay, by agency. The greater the differences, the more skewed the distribution. We see, then, that the distribution for agency three is highly skewed, while those for agencies six and eight are much less so. Since the average length of stay is usually related to both the type and severity of the physical condition, further exploration of the interrelationship of these two measures is necessary. While such analysis is beyond the scope of this book, the data presented in table 3-19 suggest the degree to which agencies differ with regard to the types of conditions for which their clientele were hospitalized.

Summary

While the sociodemographic data obtained were somewhat incomplete, the picture that emerged showed that, for the most part, the families from which the sample children derived subsisted on low income, many below the poverty level; were disproportionately black and Puerto Rican; were below average in years of schooling; and were characterized by high levels of family impairment. Maternal physical and mental illness was the dominant reason for placement. Over 40 percent of the sample had been placed more than once, and more than half had been in care four or more years.

In terms of interagency data, the following variables were found to be significant at or beyond the .05 level of confidence:

Sociodemographic	*Health*
Ethnic group	Admission health status
Religious affiliation	Abnormal findings-preventive examination
Reason for placement	
Source of referral	Chronic-serious health problems
Age at placement	Hospitalization rates, length of stay, and diagnoses
Length of time in placement	
Number of placements	

On the one hand, the measures that are primarily sociodemographic in character appear to suggest that the agencies, by virtue of their religious affiliations, administrative structures, and policies, draw their cases from

Table 3–19
Percentage Distribution of Diagnostic Conditions Causing Hospitalization of Study Children, by Agency, 1968–1973

Condition	Study Total (n = 315)	Agency One (n = 47)	Two (n = 72)	Three (n = 57)	Four (n = 21)	Five (n = 43)	Six (n = 38)	Seven (n = 19)	Eight (n = 18)
Total	100	100	100	100	100	100	100	100	100
Respiratory condition	21	17	25	23	52	12	13	5	22
Injuries	20	10	13	30	14	23	16	37	28
Battered-child syndrome	5	6	4	7	10	—	3	5	17
Other	15	4	9	23	4	23	13	32	11
Congenital anomalies	11	13	11	5	5	19	11	16	11
Orthopedic	4	—	8	2	—	14	—	—	—
Other	7	13	3	3	5	5	11	16	11
Digestive-system conditions	11	13	13	9	14	5	16	11	6
Hernia	5	—	8	5	5	2	8	5	6
Other	6	13	5	4	9	3	8	6	—
Nervous-system conditions	7	9	6	5	—	7	15	5	—
Genitourinary conditions	7	17	11	2	—	5	3	5	11
Eye conditions	5	12	6	4	5	—	8	—	—
Infective and parasitic diseases	5	—	4	9	5	9	3	5	6
Nutritional/metabolic	4	4	1	5	5	9	3	5	—
All other conditions	9	5	10	8	—	11	12	11	16

Chi square = 88.808, d.f. = 63, $p < .05$.

somewhat different subgroups of the city. On the other hand, the health variables that generated statistically significant tendencies may be related not only to differing medical profiles among agency clientele but also to varying medical-care practices and policies.

Thus, we see that approximately one out of five (21 percent) children in the study group were hospitalized during the five-year period because of a respiratory condition, but this proportion varied sharply across the agencies from a low of 5 percent (agency seven) to a high of 52 percent (agency four) (table 3-19). The relatively large number of injuries occurring among the group is reflected in the fact that fractures, burns, and child abuse comprised the second leading category, accounting for 20 percent of the conditions requiring hospitalization. Agencies varied, however, from a low of 10 percent to a high of 37 percent in this class, with agencies one and two underrepresented and agencies three and seven overrepresented. Further differences of note within this category relate to child abuse, which caused 17 percent of agency eight hospitalizations but none in agency five. All differences are significant.

The evidence indicates, then, that the various agencies are serving somewhat different subpopulations, though the pattern of the relationship between agency and subgroup is not yet clear. Many of these differences undoubtedly are related to agency policies of acceptance of certain cases. Agencies seven and eight, for example, are operated by the same municipal agency responsible for investigation of all cases of child abuse in the city.

Notes

1. New York City Department of Social Services, "Summary Analysis of Population Reports Submitted by Foster Care Agencies—Children Remaining in Care on June 30, 1974," Form M-284 (New York, 1975).

2. H.G. Birch and J.D. Gussow, *Disadvantaged Children* (New York: Grune and Stratton, 1970); Katz et al., *American Journal of Diseases of Children,* 114 (July 1967); and Eleanor Hunt, *Recent Demographic Trends and Their Effects on Maternal and Child Health Services,* Department of Health, Education, and Welfare, Health Services Mental Health Administration, 1970.

3. All disabilities and impairments recorded by record reviewers were coded according to the *International Classification of Diseases, Adapted for Use in the United States,* 8th rev., Public Health Service pub. no. 1693 (Washington, D.C., 1967). Chronic conditions were defined and categorized to comply with the guidelines established by the National Center for Health Statistics, series 10, Public Health Service pub. no. 80 (Washington, D.C.: Government Printing Office, 1973).

4 Health Status of the Children

A major objective of this study was to describe in detail the physical-and-emotional-health status of this group of foster children. To this end, direct clinical appraisals, consisting of pediatric, mental-, cognitive, and dental-health evaluations were performed on these children. The content of the examination procedures was described in chapter 2. This chapter focuses on the health data derived from this clinical survey. The findings presented here describe the general health level of the children; the physical-, mental-, and cognitive health differentials by selected demographic and socioeconomic characteristics; and interagency health differentials. Previous cautions stated regarding representativeness of this sample must continue to be observed.

General Health Levels

Six hundred sixty-eight children, or 84 percent of those eligible for testing, were screened at the New York Hospital pediatric clinic, with specific procedures administered in accordance with age-group differentials. Tables 4–1, 4–2, and 4–3 present findings related to certain physical, developmental, psychometric, psychiatric, and dental-health variables.

Physical Health and Background Characteristics

Physician's Impression of Health Status

No statistically significant differences in terms of well or other-than-well ratings emerged by sex, age, or ethnic group (table 4–4). However, boys showed slightly higher levels of problems than girls, as did children under two years old when compared with those over two. Puerto Rican children appeared to have somewhat poorer health (33 percent) than whites (24 percent) or blacks (24 percent), but differences fell just short of statistical significance.

Table 4–1
Percentage Distribution of Children Recommended for Referral
among Children Evaluated by Survey Pediatricians

Specialty-Treatment Needs	Distribution
Total children	($n = 668$)
Referred	37
Not referred	63
Referred for one condition	26
Referred for two conditions	7
Referred for three or more conditions	4
Total Referrals	($n = 343$)
Cardiac	13
Eye	12
Orthopedic	10
Psychometric	10
Speech and hearing	9
Neurologic	8
Nutritional/metabolic	6
All other	32

Table 4–2
Distribution of Chronic Physical Conditions Diagnosed by Survey
Pediatricians

Chronic Conditions	Number	Percent
Total disabilities	442	100
Musculoskeletal	103	23
Congenital anomalies	66	15
Speech conditions	57	13
Cardiovascular conditions	52	12
Eye conditions	43	10
Digestive	39	9
Nutritional/metabolic	33	7
Respiratory conditions	26	6
Nervous-system disorders	13	3
All others	10	2

Table 4–3
Selected Clinical-Survey Findings for Study Group

Type of Problem	Number of Examinees	Percent with Positive Findings
Diagnosed as other than well child[a]	668	26
Height and weight levels below fifth percentile	648	8
Laboratory-test results		
Postive tine	532	2
Abnormal hemoglobin	577	4
Visual acuity: Uncorrected		
20/40 or worse	443	22
20/70 or worse	443	11
20/200 or blind	443	4
Vision-correction status		
Inadequate[b]	66	61
Inappropriate[c]	90	29
Audiometric screening[d]	540	15
Developmental levels	279	
Abnormal/questionable		29
Psychometric: Mental maturity		
Verbal test:	390	
Retarded		13
Borderline		42
Nonverbal test:	388	
Retarded		20
Borderline		30
Need for mental-health care	179	
Moderate to severe impairment		70
Need for dental care	473	38

[a]Excludes acute infections, minor skin conditions, adverse dental problems, hearing loss, and refractive errors.

[b]Inadequate correction indicates children tested with their glasses and unable to pass the acuity test.

[c]Inappropriate correction indicates children with normal acuity levels who wear glasses.

[d]8.4 percent of this group had colds, ear discharges, or other conditions at the time of testing that may have affected test results.

Table 4–4
Health Status and Treatment Referrals Recommended for Study Group as Evaluated by Survey Physicians, by Sex, Age, and Ethnic Group

Demographic Characteristic	Total Examined		Evaluation				Recommended for Referral	
			Well-Child		Other			
	Number	Percent	Number	Percent	Number	Percent	Number	Percent
Total	668	100	497	74	171	26	244	37
Sex								
Male	330	100	239	72	91	28	126	38
Female	338	100	258	76	90	24	118	35
Age								
Under 2 years	38	100	25	66	13	34	14	37
2– 5 years	269	100	191	71	78	29	96	36
6–11 years	248	100	195	79	53	21	92	37
12 years and over	113	100	86	76	27	24	42	37
Ethnic group								
White	119	100	91	76	28	24	45	38
Black and other	430	100	326	76	28	24	154	36
Puerto Rican	119	100	80	67	39	33	45	38

Referral for Specialty Care

Table 4-4 indicates that the overall proportion of children referred for specialty treatment (37 percent) did not vary significantly by sex, age, or ethnic
group; only minor percentage-point differences within specific subclasses
emerged. This proportion also did not vary by parameters such as education
of the natural mother or reason for placement, education of the foster
mother, foster-family income, or foster-family occupational status (table
4-5).

Chronic Conditions

Our data reveal that almost half the children examined (45 percent) had at
least one chronic condition. Of these, 25 percent showed evidence of a
single condition, and 20 percent exhibited multiple disabilities. Chronic illnesses were defined in the instructions to study pediatricians as "serious
medical illnesses of a chronic nature which may impair the child's current
and future functioning." Within the sample, boys averaged 0.71 problems,
somewhat more than girls, who averaged 0.58, a difference significant at
the .05 level of confidence (table 4-6). These rates include relatively minor
conditions and more-serious ailments.

The distribution of these conditions shown in table 4-6 indicates that
the boys were more likely than girls to have congenital problems or speech
disorders; girls, however, showed above-average levels of musculoskeletal
conditions. Differences in the distribution of these conditions were not
great, however.

With respect to age, the data in table 4-6 show that the number of
chronic problems detected on the physical examinations tends to decrease as
age increases, possible indicating that such conditions were corrected for the
older group. Thus, the average number of disabilities per study child is 0.76
for those under six years, 0.57 for those between six and eleven years, and
0.50 for those twelve years and older. The distribution of such conditions
shows some variation by age—that is, children under six years were more
likely to have speech problems, cardiovascular disorders, digestive-tract
conditions, or nutritional/metabolic disabilities. Those twelve years and
older, conversely, had more musculoskeletal problems. In general, though,
age variations are not pronounced.

Table 4-6 also shows some ethnic variations in the positive findings.
The average number of disabilities per child is 0.64 for the total sample but
0.80 for white, 0.62 for black, and 0.57 for Puerto Rican children. White
children are noted to have more mental retardation, musculoskeletal disorders, congenital anomalies, and speech conditions. Black children had

Table 4–5
Study Children Recommended for Specialty Treatment, by Selected Natural-Family and Foster-Family Variables

Family Variable	Total Examined		Recommended for Referral	
	Number	Percent	Number	Percent
Total	668	100	244	37
Education level of natural mother				
Grammar school or less	122	100	49	40
Some high school	188	100	70	37
High school graduate	80	100	30	38
College or beyond	28	100	7	25
Unknown	250	100	88	35
Ethnic group of natural mother				
White	139	100	49	35
Black and other	392	100	147	38
Puerto Rican	107	100	40	37
Unknown	30	100	8	27
Public-assistance status of natural family				
Yes	295	100	122	41
No	173	100	61	35
Unknown	200	100	61	31
Education level of foster mother				
Grammar school or less	145	100	52	36
Some high school	219	10	84	38
High school graduate	163	100	57	35
College or beyond	35	100	14	40
Unknown	106	100	37	35
Ethnic group of foster mother				
White	154	100	49	32
Black and other	412	100	157	38
Puerto Rican	82	100	32	39
Unknown	20	100	6	30
Annual income of foster family				
Under $6,000	108	100	40	37
$6,000–9,999	260	100	100	38
$10,000 or more	206	100	69	33
Unknown or not reported	94	100	35	37
Occupational level of foster family				
Professional/management/ administration	85	100	28	33
Clerical/skilled, unskilled	184	100	73	40
Semi-skilled, unskilled	257	100	93	36
Unemployed	9	a	5	a
Cannot determine/not applicable	133	100	45	34

[a]Numbers too small for meaningful percentaging.

Table 4-6
Chronic Conditions among Study Children, by Sex, Age, and Ethnic Group

Condition	Total Num-ber	Total Per cent	Male Num-ber	Male Per cent	Female Num-ber	Female Per cent	Under 6 Years Num-ber	Under 6 Years Per cent	6–11 Years Num-ber	6–11 Years Per cent	12 Years and Older Num-ber	12 Years and Older Per cent	White Num-ber	White Per cent	Black and Other Num-ber	Black and Other Per cent	Puerto Rican Num-ber	Puerto Rican Per cent
Total children	667		330		337		306		248		113		117		437		111	
Mental retardation	25	4	14	4	11	3	12	4	11	4	2	2	8	7	12	3	5	4
Musculoskeletal	82	12	36	11	46	14	39	13	25	10	18	16	19	16	55	13	8	7
Congenital anomalies	57	8	42	13	15	4	29	9	18	7	10	9	15	13	34	8	8	7
Speech	57	8	35	11	22	6	33	11	19	8	5	4	24	20	21	5	12	11
Cardiovascular	50	8	27	8	23	7	27	9	15	6	8	7	11	9	34	8	5	4
Eye (Strabismus)	42	6	19	6	23	7	24	8	15	6	3	3	5	4	27	6	10	9
Digestive (Hernia, all kinds)	38	6	20	6	18	5	27	9	11	4	—	—	2	2	32	7	4	4
Nutritional/Metabolic	32	5	17	5	15	4	21	7	10	4	1	1	2	2	25	6	5	4
Respiratory	26	4	14	4	12	4	11	4	12	5	3	3	3	3	20	5	3	3
Nervous-system disorders	10	2	5	2	5	2	7	2	2	1	1	1	1	1	8	2	1	1
Hearing impairments	5	1	3	1	2	1	(—)		(3)		(2)		3	3	1	b	1	1
Neoplasms	4	1	2	1	2	1	(2)		(—)		(2)		1	1	2	1	1	1
Tuberculosis (all forms)	1	b	—	—	1	b	(—)		(—)		(1)		—	—	1	b	1	1
Total number of problems	429		234		195		141		56		56							
Average number of chronic problems	0.64		0.71		0.58		0.76		0.57		0.50		0.80		0.62		0.57	

a(Number of problems/Number of children) ×100.   bLess than 0.5 percent.

more digestive, respiratory, and nutritional/metabolic problems. For Puerto Rican children, the pattern of disabilities corresponds to the distribution for the total sample, with a few exceptions. For example, they are underrepresented in the category of musculoskeletal disorders and slightly overrepresented in the categories of speech and eye problems. Differences for the most part are not meaningful.

Height and Weight Levels

Measurements performed on study children showed their growth levels to be considerably below normative expectancies—that is, 8 percent of the total group, or twice the expected number, fell below the fifth percentile for heights and weights (see table 4–7). Moreover, one-third, as compared with an expected one-quarter, fell below the lowest quartile. Although such shifts were consistent across sex and age groups up to eleven years, those children most affected were under six. Within this age range, almost three times the predicted number (11 percent) fell below the fifth percentile. Older children in the sample more closely approximated expected levels.

Vision and Hearing

Screening tests performed on survey children revealed that just under one-fourth (22 percent) had poor visual acuity (20/40 or worse) when tested without correction. There were no striking differences by sex or ethnicity, but defective vision did increase significantly with age.

Among the children questioned as to their vision-correction status, 111 (23 percent) reported that they wore glasses, but information on the adequacy of correction was limited to 66 examinees who brought their glasses to the testing center. Of these, 61 percent, a disturbingly high proportion, were found to have inadequate correction. Data analyzed to ascertain acuity levels among children who reported they wore glasses showed that more than 29 percent had normal acuity levels and thus did not require corrective lenses.

Audiometric-screening tests were administered to study children with the following results: 85 percent passed, and 15 percent were referred for further testing (table 4–8). Differences were not significant by age or sex, but the results did vary markedly by ethnicity. Fewer Puerto Rican children (75 percent) passed the screening test than their white (82 percent) or black (88 percent) counterparts, perhaps indicating a language difficulty during the testing sessions. In addition, 8.4 percent of the 540 children tested had colds, ear discharges, or other conditions at the time of testing that may have affected test results.

Table 4-7
Height and Weight Percentile Values for Study Children, by Sex, Age, and Ethnic Group

Demographic Variables	Below Fifth				Below Ninety-fifth				Above Ninety-fifth				Total Examined			
	Height		Weight		Height		Weight		Height		Weight		Height		Weight	
	Num-ber	Per-cent	Num-ber	Per-cent	Num-ber	Per-cent	Num-ber	Per-cent	Num-ber	Per-cent	Num-ber	Per-cent	Num-ber	Per-cent	Num-ber	Per-cent
Total	52	8	54	8	605	93	599	93	43	7	38	7	648	100	647	100
Sex																
Male	30	9	24	8	296	92	295	92	24	8	24	8	320	100	319	100
Female	22	7	30	9	309	94	304	93	19	6	24	7	328	100	328	100
Age																
Under 6 years	35	11	36	12	292	95	285	94	14	5	19	6	306	100	304	100
6-11 years	15	6	15	6	223	90	222	90	25	10	26	10	248	100	248	100
12 years and over	2	2	3	3	90	96	92	97	4	4	3	3	94	100	95	100
Ethnic group																
White	9	8	10	9	111	96	111	96	5	4	5	4	116	100	116	100
Black and other	33	8	35	8	387	92	391	93	36	8	31	7	116	100	422	100
Puerto Rican	10	9	9	8	107	98	97	89	2	2	12	11	109	100	109	100

Table 4-8

Hearing-Test Results for Study Children over Three Years of Age, by Sex, Age, and Ethnic Group

Demographic Variables	Total Screened		Total Referred for Further Testing		Screened as Normal	
	Number	Percent	Number	Percent	Number	Percent
Total	540	100	82	15	458	85
Sex						
Male	268	100	44	16	224	84
Female	272	100	38	14	234	86
Age						
3–5 years	190	100	32	17	158	83
6–11 years	240	100	36	15	204	85
12 years and over	110	100	14	13	96	87
Ethnic Group						
White	95	100	17	18	78	82
Black and other	357	100	43	12	314	88
Puerto Rican	88	100	22	25	66	75

Sex and age data are not significant; $p = .01$ for ethnicity.

Dental

The dental-health status of 473 study children between the ages of three and fifteen years was evaluated by direct examination, with three primary measures of outcome provided: (1) clinician's judgment of treatment needs (none, nonurgent, or urgent) (table 4–9); (2) proportion of sample showing any evidence of dental caries (prevalence); and (3) index of DMF teeth (primary and permanent decayed untreated teeth, missing or nonfunctional teeth, and filled teeth)(table 4–10). A moderately large F (filled)/DMF ratio reflects favorably on the previous care provided, whereas a large D (decayed)/DMF ratio suggests less-satisfactory care.

Treatment Needs. Table 4–9 shows that no significant differences were demonstrated between need for dental care and sex or ethnic group. However, need levels increased significantly with advancing age, rising from 21 percent for the youngest children (three through five years) to a high of 61 percent for the oldest group evaluated (twelve through fifteen years).

Dental Decay. Our data found over half of the children examined to have one or more decayed teeth, with the level of decay rising sharply and con-

Table 4-9
Dental-Treatment Needs among Study Children, by Sex, Age, and Ethnic Group

Demographic Characteristic	Total Examined		No Treatment Needed		Treatment Needed		Urgent Treatment Needed		Nonurgent Treatment Needed	
	Number	Percent	Number	Percent	Number	Percent	Number	Percent	Number	Percent
Total	473	100	294	62	179	38	18	4	161	34
Sex										
Male	228	100	135	59	93	41	14	6	79	35
Female	245	100	159	65	86	35	4	2	82	33
Age										
3–5 years	171	100	135	79	36	21	7	4	29	17
6–11 years	202	100	119	59	82	41	6	3	76	38
12 years or over	100	100	39	39	61	61	5	5	56	56
Ethnic group										
White	77	100	51	66	26	34	5	7	21	27
Black and other	309	100	184	60	125	40	9	3	116	37

Chi-square values for sex and ethnic group are not significant; for age, $p < .001$.

sistently with age. Thus, one-third of the three-to-five-year olds, two-thirds of the six-to-eleven-year olds, and three quarters of the twelve-to-fifteen-year olds had one or more instances of caries. Decayed teeth did not vary substantially by sex or ethic group.

DMF Teeth. The mean numbers of decayed (D), missing (M), and filled (F) teeth per child varied slighty but not significantly by sex (see table 4–10). Girls had slightly higher number of DMF teeth (4.9) and filled teeth (1.98)

Table 4–10
Mean Numbers of Decayed (D), Missing (M), and Filled (F) Teeth per Study Child, by Sex, Age, Ethnic Group, and Foster-Family Characteristics

Characteristic	Mean Number of DMF Teeth	Mean Number of D Teeth	Mean Number of M Teeth	Mean Number of F Teeth	F/DMF × 100 Percent
Total	4.07	2.05	0.26	1.77	43
Sex					
Male	3.95	2.12	0.29	1.54	39
Female	4.19	1.99	0.22	1.98	47
Age					
3–5 years	1.43	1.10	0.17	0.16	11
6–11 years	4.20	2.12	0.25	1.83	44
12 years or over	8.31	3.57	0.42	4.32	52
Ethnic group					
White	4.27	1.47	0.32	2.48	58
Black	4.45	2.40	0.27	1.78	40
Puerto Rican	2.83	1.47	0.15	1.21	43
Other	0.50	0.33	—	0.17	—
Foster-family annual income					
Under $6,000	5.77	3.29	0.26	2.22	38
$6,000–$9,999	3.60	1.85	0.26	1.49	41
$10,000 and over	3.54	1.47	0.24	1.84	52
Unknown	4.53	2.44	0.28	1.81	40
Foster-family occupational level					
Professional/ managerial/ administration	3.52	1.48	0.12	1.91	54
Clerical, skilled workers	3.36	1.42	0.20	1.73	51
Semi- and un- skilled workers	4.13	2.23	0.28	1.61	39
Unemployed	6.63	3.25	1.38	2.00	30
Unknown	5.08	2.84	0.27	1.97	39

than boys (3.95 and 1.54 respectively), whereas boys averaged slightly higher levels of decayed (2.12) and missing teeth (0.29) than girls (1.99 and 0.22 respectively). Although the differences are not large, the pattern suggests more-adequate levels of dental care among girls than boys. With respect to age, there were sharp and consistent increases in the mean numbers of DMF, D, M, and F teeth with increasing years, an expected trend that corresponds with nationwide data and that also reflects the fact that older children have more permanent teeth erupted being exposed to decay for a longer period of time.

Black children had surprisingly higher levels of DMF teeth (4.45) than Puerto Rican children (2.83) and slightly higher levels than white children (4.27); they also exhibited more decayed teeth (2.40) than white (1.47) or Puerto Rican (1.47) children. White children showed higher percentages of filled teeth (58 percent) than black (40 percent) or Puerto Rican (43 percent) children.

As may be seen from table 4-10, further analyses show that the mean numbers of DMF teeth decline with rising foster-family income (from 5.77 for incomes under $6,000 to 3.54 for incomes $10,000 and over), as do mean numbers of decayed teeth (from a high of 3.29 to a low of 1.47). With respect to occupational levels, the mean numbers of untreated decayed teeth appear to decline with rising occupational levels, though the trend is not consistent. Thus, children placed in homes with unemployed foster parents showed the highest levels of decayed and missing teeth, followed by those placed in homes where the foster parents held unskilled or semiskilled jobs.

There is an expected positive correlation between increasing income and percentage of well-maintained teeth, as shown by the percentage of DMF teeth that are filled (that is, maintained). The range is from 38 percent for family incomes below $6,000 to 52 percent for income levels of $10,000 and over. The overall picture suggests that children living with more economically advantaged foster families have had more-adequate dental care and also show lower levels of need than children placed with less-advantaged families.

Developmental Levels

Developmental data were collected for 279 children who approximated the racioethnic characteristics of the total survey population. The children ranged in age from one to six years, with 88 percent between two and six. Ethnic background included 65 percent black, 15 percent white, and 20 percent Puerto Rican. Of those screened, 71 percent were judged to be normal, 19 percent were questionable, and 10 percent were abnormal in their physical, motor, perceptual, and cognitive skills. Table 4-11 shows some differ-

Table 4-11
Developmental Levels of Study Children under Six Years of Age as Evaluated by Survey Psychologists, by Sex, Age, Ethnic Group, Age at Placement, and Reason for Placement

Demographic Characteristic	Total Examined		Developmental Level							
			Abnormal		Questionable		Subtotal		Normal	
	Number	Percent	Number	Percent	Number	Percent	Number	Percent	Number	Percent
Total	279	100	27	10	54	19	81	29	198	71
Sex										
Male	140	100	13	9	34	24	47	34	93	66
Female	139	100	14	10	20	14	34	24	105	76
Age										
Under 2 years	33	100	3	9	6	18	9	27	24	73
2–6 years	246	100	24	10	48	20	72	29	174	71
Ethnic group										
White	42	100	11	26	5	12	16	38	26	62
Black and other	182	100	12	7	33	18	45	25	137	75
Puerto Rican	55	100	4	7	16	29	20	36	35	64

Age at placement										
Under 3 months	99	100	7	7	14	14	21	21	78	78
3 months to under 2 years	126	100	12	10	28	22	40	32	86	68
2 to under 6 years	44	100	7	16	8	18	15	34	29	66
Unknown	10	100	1	a	4	a	5	a	5	a
Reason for placement										
Mental illness of mother or child-caring person	52	100	2	4	11	21	13	25	39	75
Severe neglect or abuse	67	100	6	9	16	24	22	33	45	67
Physical illness or incapacity of child-caring person	65	100	6	9	10	15	16	25	49	75
Abandonment/desertion and all other types of family dysfunction	71	100	8	11	14	20	22	31	49	69
Child behavior or physical problems	3	100	3	a	—	—	3	a	—	—
Unknown	21	100	2	a	3	a	5	24	16	76

[a]Numbers too small for meaningful percentaging.

ences by sex and ethnicity in the distribution of abnormal and questionable ratings but none according to age. Male, Puerto Rican, and black children were overrepresented in the questionable category, and whites in the abnormal category, though differences fell just short of statistical significance.

Simple cross tabulations suggest no correlation between developmental level and age, sex, and ethnic group of the child. However, a regression analysis performed to examine the relationship between five background variables (sex, race, age, reason for placement, years in care) and developmental status showed reason for placement to be a significant predictor. Neither length of stay nor age at placement emerged as significant predictive variables, but cross-tabulation data, with respect to age at placement, show a slight but nonsignificant trend for abnormal and questionable ratings to increase with age at placement.

Intelligence Levels

School-age members of the study sample were tested for intelligence levels and received scores, on the average, below normative expectancies. For instance, verbally (PPVT), they averaged 87, and nonverbally (Goodenough-Harris Drawing Test), they averaged 90; the expected mean value is 100. Though nonverbal levels of intelligence did not vary by sex, age, or ethnic group (table 4-12), verbal levels did: Boys scored higher than girls, averaging 91 and 83, respectively; children in the twelve-to-fifteen-year age group averaged significantly higher scores than those in the five-to-eleven-year age group (90 as compared with 86); and whites had a mean score of 93 as contrasted with 88 for blacks and 77 for Puerto Ricans, again suggesting a language handicap for these children. An exploration of the relationship between five background variables (age, sex, race, reason for placement, and length of stay) and verbal and nonverbal intelligence levels through a regression analysis yielded only one significant F ratio—for race—further pointing to a possible language difficulty that affects the performance of some of these children.

Psychiatric Impairment

A more in-depth assessment of mental functioning was obtained by means of direct psychiatric interviews, which were completed for a subsample of 179 children ranging in age from six to fifteen years. Blacks accounted for 76 percent, whites for 20 percent, and Puerto Ricans for 4 percent of the group interviewed. The disproportionately low number of Puerto Ricans

Table 4–12
Goodenough-Harris Drawing Test and PPVT Values for Study Children Aged Five through Fifteen, by Sex, Age, and Ethnic Group

Demographic Characteristics	Mean Scores Standard Deviation	Total		Normal 110 and Above		Normal 90–109		Borderline 75–89		Retarded Below 75	
		Number	Percent	Number	Percent	Number	Percent	Number	Percent	Number	Percent
Goodenough-Harris											
Total group	90 (17.23)										
Sex											
Male	90 (18.57)	187	100	28	15	64	34	58	31	37	20
Female	90 (15.91)	199	100	21	10	81	41	57	29	40	20
Age											
5–11 years	90 (16.40)	310	100	39	13	116	37	93	30	62	20
12–15 years	89 (18.18)	76	100	10	13	29	38	22	29	15	20
Ethnic group											
White	88 (17.72)	77	100	10	13	25	32	26	34	16	21
Black and other	91 (17.40)	249	100	33	13	99	40	67	27	50	20
Puerto Rican	90 (15.95)	60	100	6	10	21	35	22	37	11	18

Table 4–12 continued

| | Mean Scores | | | Intelligence Quotients | | | | | |
| | Standard Deviation | | | 90 and Above | | 69–89 | | Below 67 | |
PPVT		Number	Percent	Number	Percent	Number	Percent	Number	Percent
Total	87 (20.82)								
Sex									
Male	91 (22.06)	190	100	102	54	68	36	20	10
Female	83 (18.89)	198	100	73	37	96	48	29	15
Age									
5–11 years	86 (19.60)	313	100	149	48	118	38	46	15
12–15 years	90 (20.28)	75	100	26	35	46	61	3	4
Ethnic group									
White	93 (18.96)	77	100	44	57	28	36	5	7
Black and other	88 (20.20)	250	100	113	45	109	44	28	11
Puerto Rican	77 (22.60)	61	100	18	30	27	44	16	26

evaluated for mental-health levels reflects the fact that the five study agencies from which the children were drawn (five agencies were chosen on the basis of expenditures in the mental-health area for mental-health evaluation) were underrepresented with regard to this ethnic group as follows:

Agency	Puerto Rican
One	3
Three	0
Five	2
Seven	11
Eight	3

Survey psychiatrists divided the children, by symptoms, into categories for well and mild, moderate, marked, and severe impairment. The results showed that only 4 percent of the group were classified as being without symptoms and that 26 percent were rated as having mild, 35 percent moderate, 25 percent marked, and 10 percent severe levels of impairment. For those with moderate symptoms, intervention is important since they are considered most vulnerable to emotional decompensation. For those with severe impairment, prevention is no longer the issue, but the treatment of an already established illness is.

Simple cross tabulations show that the mental-health status of the children did not vary by their age, sex, or ethnic group or by family variables such as educational level of the natural mother or household composition (table 4–13). However, for age at placement, children in the study who entered care in infancy were less frequently evaluated as marked to severely impaired than those placed at school age (table 4–14). Though the trend is in the expected direction, the differences lack statistical significance. With regard to reason for placement, children placed in care because of severe neglect or abuse were evaluated as being significantly more impaired than children placed for all other reasons. Length of stay did not emerge as a significant predictor of emotional health and, thus, is not tabulated.

Variations in Health Status of the Children, by Agency

A major goal of the foster-care health-evaluation study was to determine the extent to which Medicaid per capita cost differentials reflected need differentials among agency clientele. The following discussion addresses this issue and, in doing so, provides a descriptive analysis of interagency health levels and a determination of the degree to which observed differentials

Table 4-13
Mental-Health Status of Study Children as Evaluated by Survey Psychiatrists, by Sex, Age, Ethnic Group, and Selected Natural-Family Variables

| | | | Mental-Health Status | | | | | |
| | Total Examined | | Marked to Severe Impairment | | Mild to Moderate Impairment | | Well | |
Characteristic	Number	Percent	Number	Percent	Number	Percent	Number	Percent
Total	179	100	63	35	108	61	8	*
Sex								
Male	94	100	35	37	54	57	5	a
Female	85	100	28	33	54	63	3	a
Age								
6-11 years	111	100	39	35	66	60	6	a
12 years or over	68	100	24	35	41	61	2	a
Ethnic group								
White	35	100	10	29	23	65	2	a
Black and other	137	100	49	36	82	60	6	a
Puerto Rican	7	100	4	a	3	a	—	
Education level of natural mother								
Grammar school or less	29	100	11	38	18	62	—	
Some high school	45	100	13	29	28	62	4	a
High school graduate	21	100	5	24	15	71	1	a
College or beyond	8	100	3	a	5	a	—	
Unknown	76	100	31	41	42	55	3	a

Ethnic group of natural mother								
White	36	100	10	28	24	66	2	a
Black or other	125	100	46	37	73	58	6	a
Puerto Rican	7	100	4	a	3	a	—	
Unknown	11	100	3	a	8	73	—	
Natural-family public-assistance status								
Yes	66	100	29	44	33	50	4	6
No	52	100	20	38	30	58	2	4
Unknown	61	100	14	23	45	74	2	3
Natural-family household composition								
Two parents	28	100	9	32	18	64	1	4
One parent	49	100	18	37	29	59	2	4
Other	50	100	20	40	28	56	2	4
Unknown	52	100	16	31	33	63	3	6

Chi square values are not significant.

[a]Numbers too small for meaningful percentaging.

Table 4-14
Mental-Health Status, by Age at Placement and Reason for Placement

Characteristic	Total Examined		Mental-Health Status					
			Marked to Severe Impairment		Mild to Moderate Impairment		Well	
	Number	Percent	Number	Percent	Number	Percent	Number	Percent
Total	179	100	63	35	108	61	8	4
Age at placement								
Under 3 months	27	100	8	30	18	66	1	4
3 months–2 years	36	100	11	31	24	66	1	3
2–6 years	58	100	20	34	34	59	4	7
6 years or over	54	100	24	44	28	52	2	4
Unknown	4	a	—	—	4	a	—	—
Reason for placement								
Mental illness of mother or child-caring person	51	100	18	35	32	63	1	2
Severe neglect or abuse	35	100	17	49	18	51	—	—
Physical illness or incapacity of child-caring person	41	100	12	29	26	64	3	7
Abandonment, desertion, and all other types of family dysfunction	43	100	13	30	28	65	2	5
Child behavior or physical problems	1	100	1	a	—	—	—	—
Unknown	8	100	2	a	4	a	2	a

Chi square = 2.71, $p = .10$.
aNumbers too small for meaningful percentaging.

yield a meaningful pattern. The following major criteria, derived from clinical-survey data, were employed for this purpose:

Specialty-treatment referrals,

Chronic physical conditions,

Height and weight measurements,

Developmental levels,

Psychometric evaluation,

Psychiatric impairment, ratings,

Visual-acuity levels,

Hearing impairment,

Dental-treatment needs.

Specialty-Treatment Referrals

Referrals Recommended. The data in table 4–15 show that although there
were no significant variations among the agencies, examinees from agencies
one, three, and six exhibited treatment needs above the level reported for
the total sample and children from agency five showed below-average
levels. The differences were not very large, however, except for agency six,
which had half of its study children referred for specialty care.

Single versus Multiple Referrals. Children referred for medical evaluation
from agency five showed significantly fewer multiple conditions than those
referred to other facilities (p less than .05), but all other agencies exhibited
quite uniform distributions for this measure. Viewed overall, the observed
variations were not significant.

Conditions for Which Referrals Were Recommended. Conditions for
which specialty referrals were made ranged widely over a large number of
categories, with no single problem accounting for most of the total referrals
recommended.

As may be seen in table 4–15, there were variations in conditions requiring medical attention at the eight agencies. For instance, agency five had a
considerably higher proportion of cardiac referrals than the other facilities
(39 percent as compared with an overall average of 13 percent) and a lower
proportion of psychometric referrals (zero as compared with a sample mean
of 10 percent). Differentials were exhibited further with respect to eye con-

Table 4–15
Conditions for and Number of Referrals Recommended by Study Pediatricians, by Agency

Referrals and Condition	Total Examined		Agency															
			One		Two		Three		Four		Five		Six		Seven		Eight	
	Number	Per-cent	Number	Per-cent	Number	Per-cent	Number	Per-cent	Number	Per-cent	Number	Per-cent	Number	Per-cent	Number	Per-cent	Number	Per-cent
Number of referrals																		
Total	668	100	78	100	83	100	86	100	77	100	91	100	85	100	81	100	87	100
One or more	244	37	32	41	28	34	34	40	26	34	25	27	42	49	28	35	29	33
None	424	63	46	59	55	66	52	60	51	66	66	73	43	51	53	65	58	67
Number of conditions																		
Total	244	100	32	100	28	100	34	100	26	100	25	100	42	100	28	100	29	100
Single	178	73	24	75	22	79	23	68	18	69	24	96	28	67	19	68	20	69
Multiple	66	27	8	25	6	21	11	32	8	31	1	4	14	33	4	32	9	31
Type of condition																		
Total	343	100	43	100	38	100	49	100	37	100	26	100	64	100	45	100	41	100
Cardiac	46	13	7	16	5	13	3	6	1	3	10	39	7	11	8	18	5	13
Eye	41	12	2	5	6	16	11	22	6	16	4	15	5	8	4	9	3	7
Orthopedic	34	10	9	21	2	5	4	8	2	5	1	4	5	8	6	13	5	12
Psychometric	34	10	2	5	4	11	5	10	6	16	—	—	6	9	5	11	6	15
Speech and hearing	31	9	6	14	5	13	3	6	2	5	3	12	5	8	4	9	3	7
Neurologic	26	8	—	—	4	11	3	6	3	8	4	15	6	9	3	7	3	7
Nutritional/metabolic	20	6	3	7	2	5	3	6	2	5	—	—	3	5	2	4	5	12
All others	111	32	14	32	10	26	17	36	15	42	4	15	27	42	13	29	11	27

ditions and orthopedic problems. For the former, agency three was notice-ably higher than average (22 percent as compared 12 percent), and agency one was noticeably lower (5 percent); for the latter, agency one was quite above average (21 percent as against a sample mean of 10 percent).

The distribution of conditions for which medical attention might be needed is not statistically significant, and the small numbers in each category require that any minor variations be viewed with great caution since they do not seem to reflect any significant underlying factors that might differentiate the study facilities.

Chronic Physical Conditions

Although the study facilities did not vary significantly in the aggregate numbers of chronic conditions noted, they did differ considerably with regard to the types of problems identified (chi square = 86.618, p = less than .05)(table 4-16). Musculoskeletal conditions were at above-average levels at agencies one, three, and eight; congenital anomalies at agency five; speech disorders at agencies one and two; cardiovascular problems at agency one; eye conditions at agency four; and respiratory disorders at agencies three and four. The precise meaning of these differences is difficult to interpret without a matching detailed profile of each child, which lies beyond the scope of this book, but it appears that these patterns tend to reflect the differing subpopulations served by the agencies.

Height and Weight Measurements

As noted earlier, the children in our survey group fell significantly below normative expectancies for height and weight levels. Agencies two and six were below sample levels for height, and agencies three, six, and seven were below sample levels for weight (table 4-17).

Developmental Levels

With respect to interagency differences in developmental health, the proportion classified as abnormal or questionable ranged from a low of 18 percent (agency four) to a high of 44 percent (agency six), but for the sample sizes involved, the differences were not statistically significant, and the small numbers involved do not permit reliable conclusions to be drawn about interfacility variations (table 4-18).

Table 4-16
Diagnostic Categories of Chronic Conditions Identified by Survey Pediatricians, by Agency

Category	Total Conditions		One		Two		Three		Four		Five		Six		Seven		Eight	
	Num-ber	Per-cent	Num-ber	Per-cent	Num-ber	Per-cent	Num-ber	Per-cent	Num-ber	Per-cent	Num-ber	Per-cent	Num-ber	Per-cent	Num-ber	Per-cent	Num-ber	Per-cent
Total	467	100	68	100	52	100	60	100	44	100	65	100	71	100	67	100	40	100
Mental retardation	25	5	1	1	1	2	3	5	2	5	6	9	4	6	6	9	2	5
Physical disorders	442	95	67	99	51	98	57	95	42	95	59	91	67	94	61	91	38	95
Musculoskeletal	103	22	21	31	8	15	17	29	8	18	7	11	12	17	17	25	13	33
Congenital anomalies	66	14	5	7	8	15	9	15	5	11	15	23	11	15	9	13	4	10
Orthopedic	22	5	—	—	4	8	3	5	3	7	6	9	3	4	3	4	—	—
Other	44	9	5	7	4	8	6	10	2	5	9	14	8	11	6	9	4	10
Speech conditions	57	12	13	19	10	19	2	3	6	14	9	14	7	10	7	11	3	8
Cardiovascular conditions	52	11	12	18	5	10	3	5	4	9	10	15	8	11	5	7	5	1
Murmurs	44	9	8	12	5	10	3	5	4	9	10	15	5	7	4	6	5	1
Other	8	2	4	6	—	—	—	—	—	—	—	—	3	4	1	1	—	—
Eye conditions (Strabismus)	43	9	5	7	7	13	5	8	9	21	5	8	7	10	4	6	1	3
Digestive (hernia, all kinds)	39	9	6	9	3	6	4	7	1	2	6	9	7	10	8	12	4	10
Nutritional-metabolic	33	7	—	—	4	8	4	7	3	7	4	6	7	10	7	11	4	10
Respiratory conditions	26	6	3	5	4	8	8	13	5	11	1	2	3	4	—	—	2	5
All other	23	5	2	3	2	4	5	8	1	2	2	3	5	7	4	6	2	5

Chi square = 86.618, p < .05.

Table 4-17
Height and Weight Percentile Values for Study Children Clinically Examined, by Agency

Percentile Points	Total Examined	Agency							
		One	Two	Three	Four	Five	Six	Seven	Eight
Height[a]	(n = 648)	(n = 76)	(n = 82)	(n = 79)	(n = 76)	(n = 91)	(n = 84)	(n = 75)	(n = 85)
Total	100	100	100	100	100	100	100	100	100
Below fifth	8	5	12	9	5	9	11	8	5
Below twenty-fifth	33	38	37	38	29	26	40	33	24
Below seventy-fifth	81	80	80	84	82	81	87	80	75
Below ninety-fifth	93	92	96	91	93	90	96	95	93
Above ninety-fifth	7	8	4	9	7	10	4	5	7
Weight[b]	(n = 647)	(n = 75)	(n = 82)	(n = 79)	(n = 76)	(n = 90)	(n = 84)	(n = 75)	(n = 86)
Total	100	100	100	100	100	100	100	100	100
Below fifth	8	4	7	11	8	8	10	12	7
Below twenty-fifth	33	32	32	43	30	30	37	35	28
Below seventy-fifth	78	79	72	87	76	79	77	80	73
Below ninety-fifth	93	91	87	96	91	96	94	96	91
Above ninety-fifth	7	9	13	4	9	4	6	4	9

[a]F ratio = 2.730, $p < .01$.
[b]F ratio = 1.736, $p < .10$.

Table 4-18
Developmental Levels among Study Children under Six Years of Age, by Agency

Developmental Level	Total Examined		One		Two		Three		Four		Five		Six		Seven		Eight	
	Number	Per cent	Number	Per cent	Number	Per cent	Number	Per cent	Number	Per cent	Number	Per cent	Number	Per cent	Number	Per cent	Number	Per cent
Total	279	100	28	100	36	100	38	100	33	100	37	100	41	100	31	100	35	100
Normal	198	71	19	68	26	72	30	79	27	82	25	68	23	56	22	71	26	74
Abnormal	27	10	2	7	3	8	2	5	1	3	7	19	7	17	3	10	2	6
Questionable	54	19	7	25	7	20	6	16	5	15	5	13	11	27	6	19	7	20

Chi square is not significant.

Psychometric Evaluation

Verbal and nonverbal intelligence levels of school-age-sample members were ascertained using the PPVT and the Goodenough-Harris Drawing Test. The results, shown in table 4–19, reveal no significant interagency differences in this regard.

Psychiatric-Impairment Ratings

For the purposes of interagency significance testing, the five impairment categories were collapsed as well-mild-moderate and marked-severe. Viewed as such, there were variations in the proportions of marked-severe children, ranging from a low of 21 percent at agency five to a high of 48 percent at agency eight, but for the sample sizes involved, the differences were not significant.

Visual-Acuity Levels

Interagency acuity-level data show the proportion of study children with defective vision (20/40 or worse) to vary from a low of 10 percent at agency eight to a high of 32 percent at agency three. These differences were marginally significant.

The proportion of children that reported that they wear glasses or corrective lenses ranged across the agencies from a low of 15 percent (agency two) to a high of 35 percent (agency three). While these variations correspond to the pattern observed earlier for uncorrected acuity levels, the small numbers involved do not permit reliable conclusions to be drawn about interfacility differentials.

Information on the adequacy of correction was limited to the sixty-six children who brought their glasses to the examination center. (Forty-five children did not bring their glasses with them). Of these, 61 percent, as noted earlier, were found to have inadequate correction. Although the small numbers reported did not permit significance testing, the overall pattern suggests that no meaningful differences exist among agencies with respect to this parameter.

Concerning the appropriateness of correction, data were analyzed to ascertain acuity levels among the children who reported that they wear glasses. More than one-fourth of this group had normal acuity levels and, thus, did not require corrective lenses. Though, again, the numbers involved were too small to permit significance testing, the agencies seem quite similar with regard to this measure.

Table 4-19
Percentage Distribution of PPVT and Goodenough-Harris Scores for Study Children Five to Fifteen Years of Age, by Agency

Test Scores	Total Examined (n = 390)	Agency							
		One (n = 49)	Two (n = 47)	Three (n = 40)	Four (n = 57)	Five (n = 57)	Six (n = 46)	Seven (n = 40)	Eight (n = 54)
PPVT intelligence quotients									
Total	100	100	100	100	100	100	100	100	100
0-67 (retardation)	13	8	21	5	14	5	21	12	15
68-89 (borderline)	42	31	36	58	42	42	46	48	39
90 and above (normal)	45	61	43	37	44	53	33	40	46
Mean scores	87	92	87	90	86	92	81	81	85
Standard deviation (N-1)	20.8	19.1	23.6	18.8	20.2	17.4	23.2	22.7	20.4
Goodenough-Harris standard scores	(n = 388)	(n = 49)	(n = 46)	(n = 40)	(n = 56)	(n = 57)	(n = 46)	(n = 40)	(n = 54)
Total	100	100	100	100	100	100	100	100	100
90 and above (normal)	50	51	46	73	38	53	52	60	39
125 and above	4	2	4	—	2	9	2	—	7
110-124	9	10	7	8	7	18	4	18	4
90-109	37	39	35	65	29	26	46	42	28
75-89 (borderline)	30	33	32	20	41	26	24	25	33
below 75 (retarded)	20	16	22	7	21	21	24	15	28
Mean scores	90.07	90.57	89.33	94.55	86.56	93.37	87.89	91.83	87.56
Standard deviation (N-1)	17.23	17.15	16.86	10.96	15.33	20.53	16.25	14.95	20.93

Chi square is not significant.

Hearing Impairment

Proportionately, referrals recommended across the agencies ranged from a low of 7 percent (agency seven) to a high of 24 percent (agency two), but the differences were not statistically significant (table 4–20). Similarly, the distribution of children having some condition that may have affected test results at the time of the clinical examination was fairly even across the agencies. Levels of hearing impairment do not appear to vary significantly among the agencies.

Dental-Treatment Needs

Dental-treatment needs varied significantly among the agencies, with proportions ranging from a low of 16 percent (agency four) to a high of 49 percent (agencies three and six) (table 4–21). A similarly significant pattern emerged with respect to the mean numbers of decayed, missing, and filled teeth per child. Concerning emergency-treatment needs, while the numbers are too few to permit reliable conclusions, the pattern does not suggest any meaningful differences in this regard.

Summary

The health evaluations in this chapter indicate a prevalence of serious physical, mental, and developmental problems and, as such, provide some insight into the behavioral patterns and special physical-health needs of these children that are related to their growth, development, and ability to function.

The examinations of the health characteristics of foster children among the eight study agencies explored the hypothesis that health levels vary meaningfully and significantly from one facility to another.

Where the sample sizes permitted, the chi-square statistic was used to test for the significance of the differences among the agencies, and significance was found for specialty-treatment referrals for single versus multiple conditions, diagnostic categories of chronic conditions, height and weight levels, visual-acuity levels, and dental-treatment needs.

It appears, then, that some meaningful variations exist for several criteria representing common pediatric and dental-health problems; for psychiatric impairment and for those conditions that occur less frequently in child populations, significant results were not obtained. This lack of significance, however, may reflect the relatively low power of statistical tests at the sample sizes available for analysis. In general, the overall pattern sug-

Table 4–20
Audiometric-Screening Test Results among Study Children Aged Three to Fifteen Years, by Agency

Test Results	Total Examined		Agency														
			One		Two		Three		Four		Five		Six		Seven		Eight
	Number	Per cent	Number	Per cent	Number	Per cent	Number	Per cent	Number	Per cent	Number	Per cent	Number	Per cent	Number	Per cent	Number	Per cent
Total	541	100	61	100	62	100	68	100	75	100	70	100	66	100	61	100	78	100
Fail	82	15	8	13	15	24	8	12	12	16	14	20	12	18	4	7	9	12

Chi square is not significant.

Table 4-21
Dental-Referral Recommendations among Study Children Three to Fifteen Years of Age and Mean Number of Decayed (D), Missing (M), and Filled (F) Teeth per Child, by Agency

| | Total Examined | | Agency | | | | | | | | | | | | | | |
| | | | One | | Two | | Three | | Four | | Five | | Six | | Seven | | Eight | |
Treatment Status	Num-ber	Per-cent	Num-ber	Per-cent	Num-ber	Per-cent	Num-ber	Per-cent	Num-ber	Per-cent	Num-ber	Per-cent	Num-ber	Per-cent	Num-ber	Per-cent	Num-ber	Per-cent
Total	473	100	54	100	53	100	63	100	68	100	53	100	55	100	59	100	68	100
Treatment needed	179	38	17	31	25	47	31	49	11	16	25	47	27	49	25	42	18	26
Not urgent	161	34	13	24	23	43	31	49	8	12	25	47	23	42	22	37	16	23
Urgent treatment needed	18	4	4	7	2	4	—	—	3	4	—	—	4	7	3	5	2	3
D,M,F scores																		
Mean number of DMF teeth	4.07		4.89		3.02		5.51		2.26		3.51		4.67		4.95		3.93	
Mean number of D teeth	2.05		1.76		1.94		2.59		0.94		2.09		2.82		2.73		1.75	
Mean number of M teeth	0.26		0.35		0.28		0.10		0.15		0.09		0.40		0.47		0.24	
Mean number of F teeth	1.77		2.78		0.79		2.83		1.18		1.32		1.45		1.75		1.94	

Treatment chi square = 31.76, $p < .01$.

gests that health levels tend to vary from one agency to another but that interpretation of these findings requires an examination of the consistency of the differences observed across all the criteria employed—that is, are particular agencies consistently higher or lower than others with respect to the health measures utilized?

One approach to the problem can be taken by examining those agencies in which the proportions of children with problems are uniformly higher or lower than the proportions for all agencies. Thus, if we use the three major criteria for which significant differences occurred and use as a rough measure a scale of given percentage points above or below the proportions obtained for the sample totals, the following results emerge:

Criterion	Agency							
	One	Two	Three	Four	Five	Six	Seven	Eight
Height and	0	+1	+1	−1	−1	+1	0	−1
Weight levels	0	0	+1	0	0	+1	+1	−1
Visual-acuity levels	+1	−1	+1	0	0	+1	0	−1
Dental-treatment needs	−1	+1	+1	−1	+1	+1	0	−1

+1 = Percentage level five points or more above the level for the total sample;

  0 = Percentage level less than five points above or below the level for the total;

−1 = Percentage level five points or more below the level for the total sample.

Using this approach, three facilities consistently stand out—namely, agencies three and six, which appear to serve populations having uniformly higher levels of problems than the sample as a whole, and agency eight, which seems to have a case load of children with consistently lower levels of adverse health. This is, to be sure, a rough measure that must be regarded with caution, but it does suggest the possibility that the health characteristics of children in five of the eight study agencies were somewhat comparable, with two facilities exhibiting higher, and one lower, levels of need. For the most part, however, no consistent pattern of agency-related differences emerged, suggesting that the health characteristics of agency clientele are roughly comparable. To provide a context for these health profiles, chapter 5 compares these data to other studies made in New York City and elsewhere.

5 Interstudy Comparisons: The Foster-Care Health Study and Related Research

The analyses conducted so far have been primarily internal in character—that is, we have considered only the data supplied by the Foster-Care Health Study (FCHS) sample. This chapter compares these findings to other studies made in New York City and elsewhere.

The methodologic problems inherent in such an undertaking are obvious. First, there is the issue of comparability of samples. Some of the surveys are of children in foster care, whereas others concern children drawn from wider bands of the social spectrum. Second, there is the question of comparing children from New York City with those living in other communities. Finally, there is the problem of methodological differences in categorization that inevitably occur between disparate studies. These difficulties require that our comparisons be viewed cautiously.

The conceptual framework utilized in this chapter is the expectation that findings on the one hand would compare positively with other studies of children in foster care or similar situations. Where, on the other hand, the reference groups are derived from a wider socioeconomic range, we expect the levels of health problems in our group to be consistently higher.

Background Data

Several studies of children in foster care in New York City provide comparable ethnic data. New York City Department of Social Services monthly analyses of foster-care-population reports (available in 1974) show that during the fifteen years from 1959 to 1974 the ethnic composition of the city's foster boarding-home population shifted considerably, with a sharp rise in the proportions of black and Puerto Rican children and a decline in the numbers of white clientele.[1] As may be seen in table 5-1, black foster children are slightly overrepresented and whites are slightly underrepresented in the FCHS sample, reflecting differences of the agencies available for study. Thus, as noted earlier (chapter 2) one predominantly Jewish agency was dropped from consideration because its case load consisted of infants under two years of age, a range too narrow for medical and statistical purposes, and several other facilities refused cooperation. Although

Table 5-1

Percentage Distribution of Ethnic Composition and Religious Affiliation of Children in Foster Boarding-Home Care in New York City (1959–1974) and in the FCHS Sample (1973)

Demographic Characteristic	FCHS 1973	New York City Foster Boarding-Home Population 1959	1974
Ethnic group	100	100	100
White	18	44	21
Black and other	64	37	57
Puerto Rican	18	19	22
Religious affiliation			
Total	100	100	100
Catholic	46	57	47
Protestant	48	36	51
Jewish	5	7	2

Source: Bureau of Child Welfare, New York City Department of Social Services, "Summary Analysis of Monthly Population Reports Submitted by Foster Care Agencies" (New York, 1959–1974).

the percentage-point differences are not large, the FCHS data are more reflective of the characteristics associated with black children than any correlated with white and Puerto Rican children. By comparison, available national data reveal that 61 percent of the children in care in this country in 1977 were white, 29 percent were black, 4 percent were Hispanic, and 6 percent were other races, a distribution which differs markedly from both our FCHS sample and New York City's foster boarding-home population.[2] Also, and not unexpected, are the even more-pronounced ethnic differences between our sample and the U.S. general child population, which in 1977 had an ethnic composition that was 83 percent white, 15 percent black, and 2 percent other races.[3]

Related citywide data on religious composition show that there has been a steady and uninterrupted rise in the Protestant segment and a corresponding decline in the Catholic and Jewish components of the city's foster-care population.[4] FCHS religious profiles are in accord with these figures, with the discrepancies observed a function of the agencies for study and the fact that most of the black population is identified as Protestant (see table 5-1).

Numerous studies that have documented the characteristics of children in care have cited poverty and its related stresses as the main factors associated with and precipitating placement of children.[5] Thus, in 1974 in New York City, one out of two children in care came from homes dependent on welfare, and a similar proportion had been living in single-parent households.[6] FCHS data compare favorably with these figures. Although information on income was unavailable for 30 percent of our sample group, the figures obtained revealed that two out of three sample children were supported by public assistance in the year prior to the child's placement, underscoring the marginal circumstances of the study group.

Moreover, and in accord with the literature in this field, the most frequent factors contributing to the placement of the children in our study were those associated with some form of parental dysfunction. Comparable national statistics collected in 1977 show that the most important reasons for entry during that year were child neglect, unwillingness to continue care, abandonment, abuse, and parental emotional problems.[7] Similar findings have been reported for New York State's foster-care clientele. Thus, in 1978, the New York State Temporary Commission on Child Welfare reported that nearly 80 percent of those placed were in care because of parental problems, with child-related conditions accounting for only a minority of placements.[8] Related data supplied by the New York City Office of the Comptroller showed that in 1977 the parents' inability to cope was the most frequent reason given for placement of a child.[9] Taken together, the overall picture portrays a fundamental breakdown in family life. In the light of these circumstances, it is unfortunate that once placed in foster homes, these children are not always assured a stable, continuous, or secure environment. In fact, national statistics show that children in foster families have about a one in two chance of experiencing multiple placements and a one in ten chance of having four or more placements.[10] In New York State, information supplied by the Temporary Commission of Child Welfare in 1978 revealed that about half of the sample studied had lived in at least three foster homes and that over 10 percent had been placed in five or more homes.[11] Similar findings were reported for the FCHS sample group.

Not only do children in care often experience multiple placements, but also, once placed, they tend to remain in care longer than necessary. In fact, because foster placement is so costly and because the funding mechanism offers private agencies an incentive to keep youngsters in care rather than to have them adopted or returned home, this is a particularly controversial issue today. National statistics indicate that the median length of stay for children in foster care is about two and one-half years.[12]

By comparison, in New York City the average length of placement is reported to be 5.5 years and in upstate New York it is 4.5 years, figures that compare favorably the FCHS data.[13] Moreover, examination of FCHS age at admission and length of stay showed a large clustering of cases in the over-six-years-old age category, revealing a tendency for our sample children, once placed, to remain in care. The significance of these findings is highlighted by Kadushin in his extensive review of child-welfare research:

Probably as many as 25 percent of all children placed run the risk of growing up in foster care as "orphans of the living," and the longer a child is in
care, the longer he is likely to remain in care.[14]

Fanshel similarly notes that after the first year there is a rapid decline in
the discharge rate and that after three and one-half years "most of the
children then in care seem destined to spend their remaining years of childhood as foster children.[15] Apparently, for a sizable proportion of foster
children, whether in New York City or elsewhere, foster care is not a temporary expedient, and for some children the impact of prolonged substitute
care may well lead to higher levels of impairment and emotional disturbance. Fanshel poses the question: "Is it the breeding ground for the next
generation of impaired parents?"[16] A recent New York City performance
audit showed that 87 percent of a random sample of children entering
boarding homes had no major emotional or social problem at the time of
placement. However, once placed, one out of five showed marked deterio-
ration, exhibiting symptoms such as extreme anxiety, enuresis, nightmares,
and hyperactivity during their placement.[17]

Health Status

Since the Health Examination Survey (HES) clinical-examination protocols
served as the principal prototype for the design of the FCHS survey, the
form in which data have been derived in both these investigations should be
roughly comparable. Thus, in each survey, the examining pediatrician
recorded his diagnostic impression of the child's general health status—excluding from his assessment acute conditions, minor skin problems, dental
caries, defective vision and hearing, abnormal laboratory-test results or
other procedures—and assigned a rating of well or other than well—that is,
having some findings requiring further evaluation.

Our results show that the FCHS sample children appear overall to be
less healthy than those of comparable ages from nationwide HES study
groups. For example, among the six-to-eleven year olds, one child in five
had some significant finding compared with one child in nine in the HES
sample.[18] (Previous cautions regarding representativeness of the FCHS
sample remain in effect.) Relevant comparative data are supplied by Head
Start clinical studies of preschool children and by Job Corps appraisals of
high school students. For the former, rates of significant findings of 17 and
20 percent were reported for samples in California and Boston [19]; the Job
Corps figures were considerably higher, ranging from 24 to 62 percent for
adolescents in different cities.[20]

Need for Specialty Treatment

Another set of data drawn from our study that offers a useful index of
health status relates to the need for specialty treatment for a medically
significant condition. In this category the FCHS study group tended to
exhibit need levels (37.5 percent) roughly comparable to those of several
other U.S. low-income groups in Harlem (49 percent), Boston (35 percent),
and Texas (36 percent).[21] In terms of other foster children, a recent Montreal, Canada, report indicated that 40 percent of a sample of thirty-five
children in foster care had a health problem needing special attention.[22]

Chronic Conditions

We noted large differences in rates of chronic conditions between our sample population and other pediatric-survey groups. Nearly one out of two
FCHS children clinically examined (45 percent) were found to have at least
one chronic problem; of these, one in four (25 percent) showed evidence of
a single condition, whereas one in five (20 percent) exhibited multiple disabilities. In contrast, the Bureau of the Census estimates that about 10 percent of all children nationwide (aged infant to nineteen years) are handicapped by either a physical, mental, or emotional illness.[23] The rate for
comparably aged children from the U.S. National Health Survey was only
half that of our study group (23 percent).[24] Moreover, figures furnished by
other researchers as far apart as Rochester, New York[25]; Alamance County,
North Carolina[26]; and the United Kingdom,[27] though not totally consistent,
usually fall within the range of 10 and 20 percent for samples drawn from a
wide socioeconomic spectrum. Recent data for other foster-care samples are
in accord with our study findings. For instance, Schor found that three out
of four sample children in Baltimore had at least one chronic problem,[28]
and Moffatt et al., in their Montreal survey, reported a 40 percent chronic-
illness rate.[29]

Height and Weight

Physical measurements have long been used as a practical and reliable indicator of general growth and development and, as such, offer a means of
comparing the relative health of various population groups. Thus, as a
general rule, children who are heavier and taller are healthier than those
from impoverished backgrounds. Our survey group fell significantly toward
the lower end of the measurement scales when compared with commonly
used pediatric growth standards: 8 percent, or twice the expected number,

fell below the fifth percentile for heights and weights. Moreover, about one out of every three FCHS children as contrasted with the expected one out of four were below the lowest quartile.[30] Although such shifts were consistent across sex and age groups up to eleven years, those children most affected were under six years of age. Within this age range almost three times the predicted number (11 percent) fell below the fifth percentile. Older children in our sample most closely approximated the published norms. Some recently available data corroborate our findings. Schor, in his Baltimore survey, reported that 12 percent of a sample of 344 foster children fell below the fifth percentile and that one-third were below the twenty-fifth percentile.[31] Other data reported by Moffatt et al. showed that the prevalence of short stature for a sample of thirty-five children from a Montreal social-service agency was four times the expected rate.[32]

Apparently, while the growth rates of our preschool group are considerably slower than those of children from more-advantaged segments of society, those of our school-age sample show a fairly normal pattern of acceleration. Birch and Gussow point to nutritional inadequacies as the single most important factor contributing to abnormal growth rates, therefore suggesting that FCHS children, not unexpectedly, early in their lives may have somewhat deficient diets but that later in their childhood may attain a more-adequate level of nutrition.[33]

Vision and Hearing

Impairment of either vision or hearing, both of which are clearly essential for normal communication and education, can have lifelong consequence if not overcome. In our survey, tests administered to the sample group revealed that about one in four children aged six-to-eleven years and more than one in three aged twelve-to-fifteen years had poor visual acuity (20/40 or worse). Our sample group had higher positive test results than children of similar ages from the HES that used similar testing methods and evaluative criteria.[34] However, figures furnished by other investigators of disadvantaged populations are more in accord with our findings.[35]

Study children screened for hearing levels also performed less well than children from a general pediatric population: FCHS examinees aged six to eleven were three times more likely to exhibit hearing difficulties in the speech range (500; 1,000; 2,000 frequencies) than children from the HES sample who were similarly screened (3 percent as compared with 1 percent).[36] However, the FCHS rate did fall within the range reported for several groups of disadvantaged children (2.2–3 percent).[37] The FCHS level of test failure at both the speech and nonspeech frequencies was also similar— about one out of every six FCHS examinees as compared with one out of every five to eight children from other underprivileged populations.[38]

Schor's foster-care survey also produced results consistent with our data. He found positive hearing-test results for 5.5 percent of the children tested.[39]

Prevention in this area is clearly possible for some types of problems. For example, hearing difficulties caused by recurring ear infections during the early years of language development, which can significantly impair a child's ability to learn, are treatable. Early detection and effective care could prevent cases of temporary hearing damage as well as contribute to the prevention of associated learning and behavioral disorders.

Dental-Health Status

Since dental problems are associated with inadequate diet, poor oral hygiene, and a low frequency of dental visits, it is not surprising that the picture that emerges here is consistent with the pattern displayed by our study group for physical health—that is, FCHS children resemble other children from low-income backgrounds. Thus, our dental-screening examinations revealed that nearly two out of every three (63 percent) foster children between six and eleven years of age had one or more decayed teeth as contrasted with one out of four (25 percent) comparably aged children from the HES national sample.[40] The adolescents (twelve years and over) showed a similar but less-pronounced differential; three out of four (74 percent) FCHS children compared with one out of two (51 percent) HES sample cases were found to have one or more decayed teeth.[41] An earlier survey (1960) of school-age indigent children in Chicago produced the strikingly high decay rate of 97 percent,[42] while between 40 and 90 percent of the preschool Head Start children were found to have dental caries.[43] FCHS children aged six-to-eleven years averaged four times as many untreated decayed teeth per child (2.12) as their counterparts in the HES study (0.5).[44] Among the youth samples (twelve to fifteen years) a similar trend was displayed with regard to decayed teeth—FCHS, 3.57; HES, 1.7).

One further measure of dental-health levels was supplied by survey dentists in the form of recommendations for additional treatment. These evaluations showed that two-fifths of FCHS children aged six-to-eleven years and four-fifths of children aged twelve-to-fifteen years were in need of treatment for one or more dental problems. By contrast, a study of high school students from a Pittsburgh suburb produced a rate of only 30 percent for referable dental conditions.[45] Other researchers studying low-income populations have reported figures ranging from 60 to 90 percent. In summer 1966, for example, 65 percent of 1,276 preschool children enrolled in a Boston Head Start program were referred for dental care,[46] and a more-recent study found 86 percent of a sample of Harlem adolescents to be in need of treatment.[47]

In sum, comparisons with other populations consistently place the dental needs of FCHS children at levels comparable to those of other disadvantaged groups and significantly above the levels of more socially and economically representative samples. This widespread prevalence of dental decay seems to indicate that dental care has not been promptly, consistently, or adequately provided. This suggestion is supported by data from our record survey that enabled us to ascertain that nearly half (47 percent) of those children clinically evaluated as in need of treatment had not been to a dentist in the past five years. Apparently the removal of economic barriers, at least for our foster-care sample, was not sufficient to ensure adequate utilization of preventive or therapeutic dental services. Additional education of foster mothers regarding services available and an improvement in the accessibility of services undoubtedly would prove to be productive areas for future activity of program administrations.

Birth Weights and Hospitalizations

In addition to clinical data, several other FCHS statistics derived from the record survey provide insight into the health levels of the study group. In terms of low birth weight, frequency of hospitalization, or average length of hospital stay (table 5-2), the FCHS sample is consistently worse off than their counterparts in the general child population.

Moreover, available data pertaining to the leading causes of hospitalization (table 5-3) show that children in our foster-care sample were proportionately less likely to be hospitalized for respiratory conditions than children from the HES survey population and more likely to be hospitalized for injuries, digestive conditions, nervous-system disorders, eye conditions, congenital anomalies, and genitourinary problems. In addition, disabilities suggestive of past neglect or abuse or those related to congenital defects are more common causes of hospitalization among the FCHS sample children than those in the HES sample.

**Intellectual Maturity, Developmental Health Levels,
and Mental-Health Status**

The following comparative analyses are based on four sets of FCHS data drawn from the following assessments:

Verbal/nonverbal intellectual-maturity levels for all school-age study children ($n = 386$),

Developmental evaluations obtained for all preschool study children ($n = 279$),

Mental-health assessments for a randomly selected subsample of school-age children ($n = 179$).

Table 5-2

Percentage Distribution of Low Birth Weights and Hospitalizations among FCHS and National Samples

		Hospitalizations	
Sample	Low Birth Weight	Annual Rate per Child	Length of Stay in Days
FCHS	18	0.13	8 (median)
National Health Survey			
Total	8.2	0.07	5.6
White	7.1	—	5.3
Nonwhite	13.7	—	7.4

Sources: National Center for Health Statistics, *The Health of Children, 1970.* Vital and Health Statistics, PHS Pub. No. 2121, Public Health Service. (Washington, D.C.: Government Printing Office, 1970); and National Center for Health Statistics, *Current Estimates from the Health Interview Survey.* Vital and Health Statistics, Series 10, no. 95 (Washington, D.C.: Government Printing Office, 1973).

Table 5-3

Percentage Distribution of Major Conditions Causing Hospitalization among FCHS and HES National Samples

Condition	FCHS (Under 16 years)	HES (Under 17 Years)
Respiratory	21	35
Injuries	20	14
Digestive	11	10
Congenital anomalies	11	5
Nervous system	7	4
Genitourinary	7	3
Eye	5	3

Source: National Center for Health Statistics, *Age Patterns in Medical Care, Illness and Disability.* Vital and Health Statistics, Series 10, no. 70, Public Health Service (Washington, D.C.: Government Printing Office, 1969).

Intellectual Maturity

School-age members of the FCHS population showed an exceptional weakness in verbal or language areas of mental functioning. They performed far less well than the white Nashville, Tennessee, group that was used to standardize the test. FCHS mean scores were considerably lower, 87 as compared with 100, and a substantially larger proportion scored within the lower ranges (more than half, 56 percent, tested as slow or very slow as compared with 25 percent of the standardization group, and fewer children scored within the higher ranges. Further, more than twice as many FCHS children than expected (59 percent) fell below the twenty-fifth percentile (table 5-4). Because weakness in verbal functioning is believed to be the result of deprived environments, improper nutrition, and insufficient stimulation, the low performance scores obtained by our study group were expected.

Limited data are available pertaining to the PPVT I.Q.s of other disadvantaged groups, though one study by Corwin of Spanish-speaking (Mexican) children reports a mean score considerably higher than the figure obtained by FCHS Puerto Rican children—95.8 as compared with 77.4.[48] Further inferences regarding the relative verbal intelligence of our sample population may be drawn from available literature on the Wechsler Intelligence Scales for Children (WISC), a clinical test which taps language comprehension and has been shown to correlate rather well with the PPVT.[49] The mean PPVT I.Q. of FCHS black children aged five-to-fifteen years is slightly below the mean WISC I.Q. for a national sample of black children aged six-to-eleven years; 88 as contrasted with 90. The corresponding figures for white children reveal a ten-point differential—93 for our group as compared with 103 for the national sample (see table 5-5).

In terms of other foster-care groups, little data are available. However, Fanshel and Shinn reported I.Q. scores for an urban foster-care group that were in accord with our findings. In that study, the examinees performed less well on I.Q. tests than children who were part of the test-standardization groups. The mean I.Q. of those two years and under at the time of placement (tested on the Cattall Infant Scale) was 91.71; for the toddlers at entry (assessed by the Minnesota Preschool Scale), the mean verbal score was 87.71; and for school-age children at placement (tested on the WISC), the verbal I.Q. was 89.17 (see table 5-5). Fanshel reports that repeat testing over the five-year period yielded fairly stable I.Q. scores.[50]

Goodenough-Harris Drawing Test data supplied by 386 FCHS children also revealed consistently poor performance, with 75 percent falling at or below the fiftieth percentile. Relative to their peers in the general child population, these children performed far less well; four times as many sample children as their counterparts in the U.S. child population were classified as retarded, and one-third more received ratings in the borderline range. The mean standard scores for these two groups also showed a ten-point differential (see table 5-6).

In addition, FCHS findings were consistent with the results obtained for other low-income groups. The examiner manual states that children with social or emotional problems do more poorly on the test than normal

Table 5-4
Comparison of PPVT Intelligence-Quotient Scores for FCHS Sample and Original Standardization Population
(percent)

Score Values	FCHS Sample	Standardization Population
Average-very rapid learners (90 and above)	45	75
Slow learners (75–89)	32	20
Very slow learners (below 75)	23	5
Below twenty-fifth percentile	59	25

Source: For standardization-population data, Lloyd M. Dunn, *Expanded Manual for the Peabody Picture Vocabulary Test,* Circle Pines, Minn.: American Guidance Service, Inc., 1965).

Table 5-5
PPVT Intelligence Quotients for FCHS Children Compared with Verbal Intelligence-Quotient Scores for Other Study Groups, by Ethnic Group

		Ethnic Group		
Study	Total	White	Black	Puerto Rican
FCHS PPVT (5–15 years)	87	93	88	77
HES WISC	100	103	90	—
Fanshel and Shinn	89			
PPVT score 2-5 years (Minnesota Preschool)	87.71	90.88	86.02	86.98
6 years and over (WISC)	89.17	97	84.83 (Protestant) 94.32 (Catholic)	81.47

Sources: National Center for Health Statistics: *Intellectual Development of Children by Demographic and Socioeconomic Factors—United States.* Vital and Health Statistics, Series 11, no. 11, Public Health Service (Washington, D.C.: Government Printing Office, December 1971); and D. Fanshel and E.B. Shinn, *Children in Foster Care: A Longitudinal Investigation* (New York: Columbia University Press, 1978).

Table 5-6
Percentage Distribution of Nonverbal Levels of Intellectual Maturity as Measured by the Goodenough-Harris Drawing Test for the FCHS and HES Samples

	FCHS		HES	
Standard Score Values	Ages 5-11	Ages 12-15	Ages 6-11	Ages 12-17
Percentage	(100)	(100)	(100)	(100)
90 and above (normal)	50	51	75	75
75-89 (borderline)	30	29	20	20
Below 75 (retarded)	20	20	5	5
Mean standard score	90	89	100	100

Sources: National Center for Health Statistics, *Intellectual Maturity of Children as Measured by the Goodenough-Harris Drawing Test.* Vital and Health Statistics, Series 11, no. 105, Public Health Service (Washington, D.C.: Government Printing Office, December 1970), p. 33; and National Center for Health Statistics, *The Goodenough-Harris Drawing Test as a Measure of Intellectual Maturity of Youths, 12-17 years—United States.* Vital and Health Statistics, Series 11, no. 138, Public Health Service (Washington, D.C.: Government Printing Office, 1 May 1974), p. 35.

or average children of the same age. Thus, previous studies, using a variety of intelligence tests, have shown that school-age children from families of lower social strata score lower than children from families of upper social strata.[51] For instance, as may be seen in table 5-7, foster children who participated in the Fanshel and Shinn longitudinal study obtained performance scores in the below-normal range.

Developmental Health Levels

Overall and viewed within the context of related research, serious developmental delays identified by our study pediatricians seem far more prevalent among this preschool foster-care sample than among children of comparable ages living in either a middle- or lower-income environment—that is, one child in ten in the FCHS sample could not perform tasks on the DDST that were completed successfully by 90 percent of the children younger than they. This compares with one child in thirty-three in the test-standardization population[52] and in a sample of lower-income Philadelphia children.[53] Comparative figures for normal and questionable ratings were rather similar for all three study groups (table 5-8).

Although the FCHS sample appears to deviate from the norms for abnormal development levels, this finding may be related to the fact that the

Table 5-7
Nonverbal Levels of Mental Maturity for FCHS Sample and Other Study Groups, by Ethnic Group

		Ethnic Group		
Sample	Total	White	Black	Puerto Rican
FCHS				
6–15 years	90	88	91	90
Fanshel and Shinn Minnesota Preschool				
3–6 years	90.86	91.28	86.59	96.24
WISC				
6 years and over	96.45	104	98.16 (Catholic) 89.40 (Protestant)	94.31

Source: D. Fanshel and E.B. Shinn. *Children in Foster Care: A Longitudinal Investigation* (New York: Columbia Universtiy Press, 1978).

Table 5-8
Comparison of DDST Test Results for Percentages of Preschool Children in the FCHS Sample, the Denver Standardization Sample, and a Philadelphia Low-Income Population

Developmental Level	FCHS	Denver Standardization[a]	Philadelphia[b]
Normal	71	74	74–76
Abnormal	10	3	1–3
Questionable	19	23	23

Sources: W.K. Frankenburg and J.B. Dodds, *The Denver Developmental Screening Test Manual* (Denver: University of Colorado Medical Center, 1968); and L. Sandler et al., *Developmental Test Performance and Behavioral Styles of Disadvantaged Nursery School Children* (Philadelphia: Hahnemann Medical College, 1971).
[a]Sample of white, middle-income children.
[b]Sample of low-income, black children.

previous studies were based on standardization populations that excluded as high risk children who were adopted, had been born prematurely, were breech deliveries, were twins, had serious handicapping conditions, or lacked a father.[54] Also, the Colorado standardization group included a significantly higher proportion of children whose fathers were in professional, managerial, and sales occupations than children whose fathers were in skilled-or-unskilled-labor positions or unemployed. The ethnic distribution of that population was 17 percent black and 83 percent white. Inasmuch as advantaged children have been found to perform many language items on the DDST sooner than less-advantaged children whose fathers are in the blue-collar range, it is in line with our expectations that they would perform better than their less-advantaged peers, particularly in the language section.[55] It is not surprising, then, that of the four areas measured by the DDST, language performance was the weakest for this preschool foster-care group.

Mental-Health Status

Children in our study population who were evaluated clinically by psychiatrists appear to be far more impaired mentally than children from other survey groups that received similar standardized evaluations. (See chapter 2 for a description of the clinical-evaluation procedure.) The rate of moderate to severe psychiatric impairment for the FCHS group (35 percent) is 50 percent greater than that of the Langner welfare sample (23 percent) and about triple that of his cross-sectioned group (12 percent). [The Langner samples (1972) were six-to-eighteen-year olds—a Manhattan cross section of 1,034 children, and a Manhattan welfare group of 1,000 children.][56] A clinical study of 168 six-to-seven-year-old children from Manhattan's Lower East Side (with a racial composition of 79 percent white, 12 percent black, and 9 percent Puerto Rican) by Silver and Hagan produced a figure (10 percent) comparable to Langner's.[57] However, Rutter, Tizard, and Whitmore report a prevalence rate of only 7 percent for clinically significant conditions among all ten-to-eleven-year-old children from the Isle of Wight.[58] Contrasting data for other foster-care populations are in accord with our findings. Fanshell and Shinn's examining psychologists found one in four foster children to be emotionally maladjusted five years after placement, noting that 25 percent of those "who experience care for at least 90 days will tend to show a pervasive pattern of emotional disturbance over a 5 year period."[59] For his Baltimore 1978–1979 sample, Schor reported that 37 percent of those foster childen assessed had psychological and behavioral problems. Moreover, 43 percent of the sample required referral for psychiatric services.[60] Shah, in Canada, (1972) found that one in five foster children coming into care had psychiatric disorders as their principal presenting problem and that an additional 11 percent manifested these conditions as secondary to physical illnesses.[61]

Since most of the research on the behavioral adjustment of children has been based on parent, teacher, or self-ratings, published data are not strictly comparable with our survey. Nonetheless, to the extent that these studies provide rough estimates of the level of maladjustment in contrasting populations, they are useful and instructive for comparisons. Leighton et al., using a self-administered questionnaire, found 22 percent of a North Carolina elementary school group and 17 percent of a junior-senior high school sample to be maladjusted.[62] Similar rates were reported by Lapouse for her Buffalo study group and by Pless and Roghmann in a Rochester sample of six-to-ten-year olds.[63] However, Rutter, Tizard, and Whitmore, using parent and teacher ratings, produced a rate of only 7 percent in their Isle of Wight survey,[64] and the U.K. National Child Development Study showed a similar figure (9 percent) for its sample of ordinary children.[65] It is not surprising that disadvantaged children in this same U.K. study were three times more likely than their ordinary counterparts to be classified as maladjusted (26 percent as against 9 percent). For foster children, the Fanshel and Shinn investigators report that teacher, parent, and caseworker ratings of emotional impairment fell within the 25–33 percent range.[66] A Massachusetts study of children who experienced foster care indicated that behavioral/emotional disorders were the leading single cause of illness among a sample of 5,862 children, accounting for one-third of all disabilities as reported by social workers.[67] Langner et al., in their survey of Manhattan children, found that the separation of children from their parents had a fairly strong relationship to total impairment. Thus, one out of five children who had not been consistently in their mother's care since birth evidenced impairment, compared with only 12 percent of those who had always been in her care.[68] In a related study conducted on the Isle of Wight and in a London borough, Wolkind and Rutter reported a statistically significant association between period in care and behavioral disturbance as shown both at home and at school. In that investigation, 13 percent of the Isle of Wight group and 10 percent of the children from an inner London borough were evaluated as deviant by their teachers.[69] Shah, in a one-year survey of the in-care population in Vancouver, reported that one child in ten displayed symptoms of emotional impairment. Of these, the majority exhibited conditions suggesting moderate or severe disorders, and "many had become too uncontrollable for caretakers to cope with."[70]

The methods of these studies and ours were too different for the results to be directly comparable. However, the evidence strongly suggests that children in our foster-care sample are more likely to experience behavioral maladjustment than children drawn from different broad-based populations. This impression is supported further by ratings obtained from FCHS psychiatrists pertaining to specific areas of impairment as well as behavioral information supplied by a subgroup of foster mothers ($n = 256$) questioned during personal interviews. Thus, in table 5–9, we see that the FCHS group contains nearly two times as many children having moderate-to-severe ($3 +$)

Table 5-9
**Percentage Distribution of Impairment Ratings for New York City
Children from FCHS and a Cross Section of Low-Income, High-Income,
and Welfare Samples**

Impairment Ratings	FCHS	Low Income			High Income	Total Sample
		Welfare	Nonwelfare	Subtotal		
Total (4+)	35	16	18	17	10	13
Development (3+)	45	36	26	28	22	24
School functioning (3+)	49	32	21	23	8	15
Peer relationships (3+)	48	36	33	34	20	25
Sibling relationships (3+)	36	25	12	15	20	18
Symptom (4+)	31	20	17	18	10	12
Self-confidence (4+)	29	12	12	12	6	8

Sources: T. Langner "Psychiatric Impairment in Urban Children over Time," Unpublished summary of work on project, Columbia University, May 1972; and T. Langner et al., "Children of the City: Affluence, Poverty, Mental Health," in *Psychological Factors in Poverty,* Vernon L. Allen (ed.) (Chicago, Ill.: Markham Publishing Company, 1970).

developmental impairment as the Langner et al. cross-sectional group (45 percent as against 24 percent). Langner's welfare sample shows a fairly close resemblance to our foster-care group (36 percent had 3+ ratings), but the high-income youngsters from that study display some reduction of 3+ impairment in this sphere (22 percent). In terms of 4+ ratings, 29 percent of our group fell in this category. Thus, nearly one in ten FCHS examinees were described as having one or more serious defects in functioning related to their intellectual development (for example, poor concentration, slow thinking); social behavior (for example, isolation); and physical growth. By contrast, between 4 and 7 percent of Langner's broad-based samples received 4+ ratings in this sphere, but low-income boys from that study were similar to our examinees in this regard (9 percent received 4+ ratings).[71] Although not strictly comparable, it should be noted that psychologists in the Fanshel and Shinn study, using figure drawings as a diagnostic tool, evaluated one-third of the sample as immature and one-fifth as poorly related socially. Fifty-two percent were considered somewhat related socially, and only 22 percent were seen as well-related in that study. Also noteworthy is the finding that nearly half of that foster-care sample was viewed as socially immature by their teachers.[72]

The extent of FCHS respondent awareness of developmentally related problems among their study children was revealed in answers to inquiries made during personal interviews. Thus, 20 percent of the mothers commented that their foster child was slow mentally or slow in development (as compared with 4 percent reported for a national sample[73]), 20 percent observed that their foster child had trouble remembering things, and between 4 and 6 percent cited concern over the foster child's social behavior.

For the rating of school impairment, provided by FCHS psychiatrists, the proportion of children with moderate-severe problems was more than three times as high in the foster-care group (49 percent) as in the Langner et al. cross-sectional sample (15 percent). Few high-income children from the Langner et al. survey were classified in the 3 + category (8 percent), but a disproportionate number of welfare children received this rating (32 percent)—not as many as the foster care, however.[74] In a related analysis, Langner reported that serious problems were more prevalent among low-income teenage boys, children not always in their mother's care, and children who had moved frequently, three characteristics associated with foster-care placement.[75] In addition, evidence from a broad-based nationwide survey showed markedly lower levels of school impairment among children from the general child population as compared with children from this foster-care sample or Langner's low-income and welfare groups. Thus, only 17 percent of the participants in the HES between six and eleven years and 14 percent of those between twelve and seventeen years were considered to be emotionally maladjusted to some degree. The rates for serious school impairment (suggesting disruptive, aggressive behavior; poor peer relations; and problems in academic performance) showed similar differentials: 1.4 percent for the national group compared with 7 percent for our foster-care sample.[76] By comparison, Fanshel and Shinn report that 24 percent of their study group were seen as poorly adjusted and 7 percent as very poorly adjusted by their teachers. Some of the major problems cited included poor work-study habits (43.7 percent), inability to follow class routines (25.3 percent), difficulties in comprehension (34.9 percent), and little motivation to learn (36.3 percent). In addition, about one-third of that sample received negative evaluations with respect to impulsiveness, irritability, and insecurities.[77]

In a related vein, FCHS foster mothers, in response to several questions concerning the school adjustment of their study children, reported that 10 percent had been expelled or suspended from school, 14 percent had not been promoted each year from grade to grade, and 29 percent exhibited aggressive behavior—that is, teasing and bullying other children. The rate reported by natural parents of children that returned home in the Fanshel and Shinn study was 23.4 percent for aggressive behavior, whereas the national-sample figure in this area was significantly lower, 6 percent. Eighteen percent of the FCHS sample was also considered to be troublesome in terms of discipline as compared with 7 percent of the six-to-eleven-year olds and 3.3 percent of the twelve-to-seventeen-year olds in the national survey. By contrast, teachers in the Fanshel and Shinn study assigned negative ratings in this area to 28 percent of that sample five years after entering care.[78]

Relationships outside the school also were assessed, with the following results. Forty-eight percent of the FCHS sample received 3 + ratings for peer relationships as compared with 25 percent of the Langner et al. cross-sectional sample, 20 percent of that high-income sample, and 36 percent of that welfare group.[79] With respect to 4 + ratings, 11 percent of our sample fell in this category. Parallel data provided by FCHS foster-mother respondents showed that between 5 and 15 percent were concerned about their study child's functioning in this regard.

Six percent said that their foster child had no close friends. This compares with 4.3 percent of Fanshel and Shinn's foster group that returned home at the end of five years in care. In addition, 36 percent of our sample were said to have only a few close friends, and this was true of 31 percent of Fanshel and Shinn's foster-care sample.[80]

Six percent of the FCHS respondents also reported that their foster child spends too much time alone, 4 percent rated their child as withdrawn, and 5 percent said that he or she has poor social relationships. In Fanshel and Shinn's study, caseworker ratings of children remaining in care at the end of five years revealed that "4.6 percent were usually avoided" by other children. However, for the foster-care children that returned home in that study, 12.6 percent were said by their natural parents to be excluded by other children and 21.2 percent were said to be afraid of other children. In addition, further data from that study showed that 26.8 percent of the sample rated after five years in care were viewed by their teachers as having problems in the area of peer relationships.[81] By comparison, national statistics indicate that only 1 percent of a representative sample of twelve-to-seventeen-year olds were reported by their parents to have difficulty making friends.[82]

For sibling relationships, the proportion of 3 + ratings was twice as great for the foster-care group as for the Langner Manhattan cross-sectional sample (36 percent compared with 18 percent).[83] Welfare children from the Langner et al. study again exhibited elevated impairment levels (36 percent), with the opposite trend displayed by high-income (20 percent) and cross-sectional children from that survey (25 percent).[84] In terms of marked-severe-impairment ratings, 8 percent of our sample fell in this category.

Each child also received a rating of impairment associated with symptoms such as fighting, temper loss, and isolation that was based on the number of areas of functioning affected (for example, developmental status, school adjustment, peer acceptance) and the amount of distortion to the child's life by these symptoms. In this sphere, a minimal or mild rating suggests no or few symptoms in a restricted area of the child's life, with no effect or only a mild influence on functioning. The child is either free from disabling impairment or the difficulties present are tangible but have not gotten to the point of necessitating therapeutic intervention; 32 percent fell in these two categories. Marked or severe impairment (4 + ratings), however, indicate many symptoms in almost all areas of functioning, creating a major handicap or perhaps limiting the child's functioning to a special setting; 31 percent of the FCHS sample fell in this category. This figure compares with 12 percent of Langner et al.'s cross-sectional sample and 30 percent of the welfare group.[85] Parallel data obtained from FCHS foster mothers revealed major concerns for symptoms falling in the categories of frequent restless behavior (24 percent); unusual movements, jerks, and twitches (11 percent); and touchy, moody behavior (12 percent). In comparison, data for a national sample revealed that 4 percent of a representative group of youths were considered to be very nervous by their parents.[86] For foster children, the Fanshel and Shinn study reported that 17.9 percent of the children who remained in care were evaluated by caseworkers as frequently overactive, 13 percent were rated as often tense, and 8 percent were reported to have unusual tics and movements. Of the group of children that returned home, 13 percent were viewed as often under a strain, 19 percent as quite nervous, and 25.7 percent as very excitable.[87]

The final impairment rating provided by FCHS psychiatrists, in the area of self-confidence (a measure of ego strength and self-confidence), produced the following results: 29 percent of our sample received 4 + ratings, and another 39 percent had moderate impairment in this regard. By contrast, only 8 percent of the Langner et al. cross-sectional group, 6 percent of their high-income group sample, and 12 percent of their welfare group received 4 + ratings in this category.[88] Data provided by Fanshel and Shinn's contrasting sample of foster children showed that half of that group (evaluated by figure drawings) were found to have little self-confidence.[89]

Summary

This chapter examined the background characteristics, physical health, and emotional functioning of preschool and school-age children in the study sample within the context of previously published literature. Because self-selection factors in this investigation resulted in a biased study group, it is not possible to generalize that the health status of the typical foster child is similar to that of the typical child who participated in this survey. Mindful of these limitations, however, it may be stated that the information gathered highlights the diversity of behavior and adjustment among the study children and suggests that children in our sample group of all ages are less healthy than children from other pediatric populations representing different social, cultural, and economic strata. They seem more likely to exhibit physical, emotional, and dental pathology than children drawn from broader-based samples, and it is not surprising that their needs are at levels roughly comparable to those of other disadvantaged populations.

While school achievement is not a direct indicator of health status, behavioral and adjustment problems and poor cognitive skills are correlated with developmental attrition as well as poor mental health. Moreover, for children between six and twelve years of age, "the line between mental health problems and school learning problems is often difficult to discern. . . . [R]eading and learning problems frequently lead to serious emotional and behavioral disturbances. Primary emotional disorders may lead to difficulties in reading and learning."[90] Consequently, it is important for prevention and intervention strategies to consider the multiplicity of forces involved and their interrelationships.

Finally, the greater health risks associated with poor, inner-city minority-group children are characteristic of our sample. Even bearing in mind the words of Fanshel that "the one-time cross-sectional investigation tends to be biased in the direction of finding severe pathology." it nevertheless remains true that children who stay in the foster-care system continue to have significant medical and psychiatric problems that social agencies must meet.[91]

Notes

1. Bureau of Child Welfare, New York City Department of Social Services, "Summary Analysis of Monthly Population Reports Submitted by Foster Care Agencies," (New York, 1959–1974).

2. Ann W. Shyne and Anita G. Schroeder, "National Study of Social Services to Children and Their Families," DHEW pub. no. (OHDS) 78–30150 (Washington, D.C.: U.S. Children's Bureau, 1978).

3. Ibid.

4. Bureau of Child Welfare, "Summary Analysis."

5. Shirley Jenkins, "Duration of Foster Care: Some Relevant Antecedent Variables," *Child Welfare* 46 (1967):450–455; Shirley Jenkins and Elaine Norman, "Families of Children in Foster Care," *Children* 16 (1969): 155–159.; Shirley Jenkins and Mignon Sauber, *Paths to Child Placement: Family Situations Prior to Foster Care* (New York: Community Council of Greater New York, 1966); and Governor's Commission on Adoption and Foster Care, "Report to Governor Sargent," Pub. no. 6847–14–500–6–73–Cr (Boston, March 14, 1973).

6. Trude Lash and Heidi Sigal, *The Status of the Child: New York City* (New York: Foundation for Child Development, 1976).

7. Shyne and Schroeder, "National Study of Social Services to Children."

8. Joseph Pisani, *Foster Care Reimbursement: A New Approach* (New York: Temporary State Commission on Child Welfare, 1978).

9. George Strauss, *The Children Are Waiting: The Failure to Achieve Permanence for Foster Care Children in New York City,* (Report prepared for the New York City Comptroller's Office, 1977).

10. Shyne and Schroeder, "National Study of Social Services to Children."

11. Pisani, *Foster Care Reimbursement.*

12. Shyne and Schroeder "National Study of Social Services to Children."

13. Virginia Hayes Sibbison and John McGowan, *New York State Children in Foster Care: Executive Summary* (New York: Welfare Research Inc., 1977).

14. Alfred Kadushin, "Child Welfare," in *Research in the Social Services: A Five-Year Review,* ed. Henry S. Maas (New York: National Association of Social Workers, 1971), p. 46.

15. David Fanshel, "The Exit of Children from Foster Care," *Child Welfare* no. 2 (1971), pp. 66, 77–78, 80.

16. Ibid.

17. Strauss, *The Children Are Waiting.*

18. National Center for Health Statistics, *Examination and Health History Findings among Children and Youth, 6-17 Years, United States,* Vital and Health Statistics Series 11, no. 129, DHEW pub. no. (HRA) 74–1611 (Washington, D.C.: Health Resources Administration, November 1973). Children aged six to eleven were examined from 1963 to 1965, those aged twelve to seventeen were examined from 1966 to 1970.

19. A. Gilbert, A. Lewis, and R.W. Day, "Project Head Start, An Evaluation of Medical Components in California," *California Medicine* 106 (May 1967):382–387. Sample is preschool children, primarily but not exclusively underprivileged; and R. Mico, "A Look at the Health of Boston's Headstart Children," *Journal of School Health* 36 (1966): 241–244. Sample includes 1,467 underprivileged preschool children.

20. V. Eisner, C.B. Goodlett, and M.B. Driver, "Health of Enrollees in Neighborhood Youth Corps," *Pediatrics* 38 (1966):40–43; Betty J. Bernstein "Examination of Health Aspects in the Early Planning of the Poverty Program in New York City (Paper presented at annual meeting of the American Public Health Association, Chicago, 1965); and "Major Ailments Affect One-Third of Poor Children," *Medical World News,* November 5, 1965, pp. 64–65.

21. A.F. Brunswick and E. Josephson, "Adolescent Health in Harlem," *American Journal of Public Health,* October 1972 (suppl.); Mico, "A Look at the Health"; and "Welfare Youth Get Health Test," *The New York Times,* September 1974.

22. Michael Moffatt et al., "Medical Care of Foster Children in Care of One Social Service Agency," pub. no. 000000 (Montreal: Montreal Children's Hospital Research Institute, 1982).

23. U.S. Department of Commerce, Bureau of the Census, "Handicapped Children, by Type, 1974-1975," in *Statistical Abstract of the U.S., 1977,* 98th ed. (Washington, D.C.: Government Printing Office, 1977), p. 352.

24. National Center for Health Statistics, *Children and Youth, Selected Health Characteristics—United States,* Vital and Health Statistics Series 10, no. 62 (Washington, D.C.: Health Services and Mental Health Administration, February 1971).

25. I.B. Pless and K.J. Roghmann, "Chronic Illness and its Consequence: Observations Based on Three Epidemiologic Surveys," *Journal of Pediatrics* 79 (September 1971):351-359.

26. W.P. Richardson, A.C. Higgins, and R.C. Ames, *The Handicapped Children of Alamance County, North Carolina: A Medical and Sociological Study* (Wilmington, Del.: Nemours Foundation, 1965).

27. J.W.B. Douglas, *The Home and the School* (London: Mackgibbon and Kee, 1964).

28. E.L. Schor, "The Foster Care System of Health Status of Foster Children," *Pediatrics* 69 (May 1982).

29. Moffatt, "Medical Care of Foster Children."

30. Harold C. Stuart et al., "Anthropometric Charts Based on Repeated Measurements of Children under Comprehensive Studies of Health and Development" (Boston: Children's Medical Center, Department of Maternal and Child Health, Harvard School of Public Health).

31. Douglas, *The Home and the School.*

32. Moffatt, "Medical Care of Foster Children."

33. H.G. Birch and J.D. Gussow, *Disadvantaged Children: Health, Nutrition and School Failure* (New York: Harcourt, Brace & World, Grune & Stratton, 1970), p. 184.

34. National Center for Health Statistics, *Binocular Visual Acuity of Children: Demographic and Socioeconomic Characteristics—United States,* Vital and Health Statistics Series 11, no. 112 (Washington, D.C.: Public Health Service, 1972); and National Center for Health Statistics, *Visual Acuity of Youths 12-17 Years—United States,* Vital and Health Statistics Series 11, no. 127, Public Health Service (Washington, D.C.: Government Printing Office, 1973).

35. Brunswick and Josephson, "Adolescent Health in Harlem"; and

D.M. Kessner, C.K. Snow, and J. Singer, *Assessment of Medical Care for Children*, Contrasts in Health Status, vol. 3 (Washington, D.C.: National Academy of Sciences, 1974).

36. National Center for Health Statistics, *Hearing Levels of Children by Age and Sex—United States*, Vital and Health Statistics Series 11, no. 102, Public Health Service (Washington, D.C.: Government Printing Office, February 1970).

37. Kessner et al., *Assessment of Medical Care;* and Peter Wedge and Hilary Brosser, *Born to Fail* (London: Arrow Books, Ltd., 1979).

38. Kessner et al., *Assessment of Medical Care;* and Comprehensive Health Care Projects for Children and Youth, "Systems Development Project," Report Series no. 13, (January–March 1971).

39. Schor, "The Foster Care System."

40. National Center for Health Statistics, *Decayed, Missing and Filled Teeth among Children—United States*, Vital and Health Statistics Series 11, no. 106, Health Service and Mental Health Administration (Washington, D.C.: Government Printing Office, October 1974).

41. National Center for Health Statistics, *Decayed, Missing and Filled Teeth among Youths—12-17 Years—United States*, Vital and Health Statistics Series 11, no. 144, Health Resources Administration (Washington, D.C.: Government Printing Office, October 1974).

42. Chicago Indigent Dental Survey, 1960 [Reported in Chicago Board of Health, *Preliminary Report on Patterns of Medical and Dental Care in Poverty Areas of Chicago and Proposed Health Programs for the Medically Indigent* (Chicago, 1965)].

43. A.F. North, "Project Head Start and the Pediatrician," *Clinical Pediatrics* 6 (April 1967):191-194.

44. National Center for Health Statistics, *Decayed, Missing and Filled Teeth.*

45. K.D. Rogers and G. Reese, "Health Studies of Presumably Normal High School Students," *American Journal of Diseases of Children* 108 (December 1964):572-600.

46. Mico, "A Look at the Health."

47. Brunswick and Josephson, "Adolescent Health in Harlem."

48. Betty J. Corwin, "The Influence of Culture and Language on Performance on Individual Ability Tests," Unpublished study (Northridge, Calif.: San Francisco Valley State College, Div. Educ., 1962).

49. J. Iavitt, "Comparison of the Peabody, Wechsler, Binet and California Tests of Intellectual Ability among 7th to 9th Grade Pupils," Unpublished paper (Westfield, Mass.: Westfield Public Schools, 1963); A.E. Lindstrom, "A Comparison of the Peabody Picture Vocabulary Test and the Wechsler Intelligence Scale for Children," *Studies in Minnesota Education* (1961), pp. 131-132; and P. Himelstein and J.D. Herndon,

"Comparison of the WISC and PPVT with Emotionally Disturbed Children," *Journal of Clinical Psychology* (1962) p. 82.

50. D. Fanshel and E.B. Shinn, *Children in Foster Care: A Longitudinal Investigation* (New York: Columbia University Press, 1978).

51. D.B. Harris, *Children's Drawings as Measures of Intellectual Maturity* (New York: Harcourt, Brace & World, 1963).

52. W.K. Frankenburg et al., "The Revised Denver Developmental Screening Test: Its Accuracy as a Screening Instrument," *Journal of Pediatrics* 59 (December 1971):6.

53. L. Sandler et al., *Developmental Test Performance and Behavioral Styles of Disadvantaged Nursery School Children* (Philadelphia: Hahnemann Medical College, 1971).

54. Ratings, according to the test developers, have a referral criterion designed to correspond to I.Q.s or D.Q.s (developmental quotients). See W.K. Frankenburg et al., "Development of Preschool Aged Children— Racial, Ethnic and Social Class Comparisons" (Presented to SCRD meeting, Philadelphia, March 1973).

55. W.K. Frankenburg and J.B. Dodds, *The Denver Developmental Screening Test Manual* (Denver: University of Colorado Medical Center, 1968).

56. T. Langner, "Psychiatric Impairment in Urban Children over Time," Unpublished summary of work on project, Columbia University, May 1972.

57. A. Silver and R. Hagan, "Profile of a First Grade: A Basis for Preventive Psychiatry," *Journal of the American Academy of Child Psychiatry* 11 (October 1972):695-774.

58. M. Rutter, J. Tizard, and K. Whitmore, *Education Health and Behavior* (London: Longmans, Green, 1970).

59. Fanshel and Shinn, *Children in Foster Care.*

60. Schor, "The Foster Care System."

61. C.P. Shah, "The Value of Admission Medical in Child Welfare," *Ontario Association of Children's Aid Societies Journal* 15 (November 19, 1972).

62. L. Leighton et al., "Measuring Stress Levels of School Children as a Program Monitoring Device: Three Years Experience in a Single School System. 1969, 1971, 1972." (Unpublished study).

63. R. Lapouse, "Relationship of Behavior to Adjustment in a Representative Sample of Children," *American Journal of Public Health* 55 (1965):30-41; Lapouse, "Epidemiology of Behavior Disorders in Children," *American Journal of Disabled Children* 3 (1966):594-599; and Pless and Roghmann, "Chronic Illness."

64. Rutter et al., *Education, Health, and Behavior.*

65. Wedge and Brosser, *Born to Fail.*

66. Fanshel and Shinn, *Children in Foster Care.*

67. Governors Commission on Adoption and Foster Care, "Report to Governor Sargent."

68. Langner, "Psychiatric Impairment in Urban Children."

69. S. Wolkind and M. Rutter, "Children Who Have Been in Care: An Epidemiological Study," *Journal of Child Psychology and Psychiatry* 14 (1973):97–105.

70. C.P. Shah, "Psychiatric Consultations in a Child Welfare Agency: Some Facts and Figures," *Canadian Psychiatric Association Journal* 19 (1974):393–397.

71. Langner, "Psychiatric Impairment."

72. Fanshel and Shinn, *Children in Foster Care.*

73. National Center for Health Statistics, *Parent Ratings of Behavioral Patterns of Youths 12–17 Years—United States,* Vital and Health Statistics Series 11, no. 137, DHEW pub. no. (HRA) 74–1619, Health Resources Administration (Washington, D.C.: Government Printing Office, May 1974).

74. Langner, "Children of the City."

75. Langner, "Psychiatric Impairment."

76. National Center for Health Statistics, *Behavior Patterns in School,* Vital Statistics Series 11, no. 139, Public Health Service (Washington, D.C.: Government Printing Office, May 1974).

77. Fanshel and Shinn, *Children in Foster Care.*

78. Ibid.; and National Center for Health Statistics, *Behavior Patterns in School.*

79. Langner, "Psychiatric Impairment."

80. Fanshel and Shinn, *Children in Foster Care.*

81. Ibid.

82. National Center for Health Statistics, *Parent Ratings of Behavioral Patterns.*

83. Langner, "Psychiatric Impairment."

84. Langner et al., "Psychiatric Impairment in Welfare"; and Langner et al., "Children of the City."

85. Ibid.

86. National Center for Health Statistics, *Parent Ratings of Behavioral Patterns.*

87. Fanshel and Shinn, *Children in Foster Care.*

88. Langner et al., "Psychiatric Impairment in Welfare"; and Langner et al., "Children of the City."

89. Fanshel and Shinn, *Children in Foster Care.*

90. Wolkind and Rutter, "Children Who Have Been."

91. Fanshel and Shinn, *Children in Foster Care.*

6 Health Services for Foster Children

This country has been committed to meeting the health requirements of its needy children for almost half a century, with the gamut of services currently encompassing preventive, disgnostic, and treatment programs, as well as counseling. For these children, such services are provided through Title XIX Medicaid funds that are allocated to cover the cost of routine medical care and treatment services for vision, hearing, and other physical problems that are more prevalent among the disadvantaged than the general population. That money and services are available does not, however, ensure that these children obtain the services they need to keep them well or that the services have been integrated, coordinated, or adequate.

This chapter examines the extent to which medical, dental, and mental-health services have been made available to the sampled subgroup of New York City's foster-care population. The findings have been drawn from several sets of data gathered during this investigation, as described in the next section.

Various methods exist for appraising health-care systems. These range from clinical-record review, observation of physicians' activities, examination of utilization statistics, and evaluation of outcome measures to direct personal interviews with administrative and professional medical staff. Emphasis may be on administrative-organizational effectiveness, patient-oriented effectiveness, cost-effectiveness, or all of these. Moreover, performance may be determined by how closely certain well-defined levels of service are attained. For example, the type and frequency of immunization tests performed may be compared with standards that indicate the optimum, or the reported number of visits for well-baby care may be compared with the optimum number of visits. Our methodologic approach for assessing agency operations—that is, organization, staffing and control systems, allocation of resources, and cost factors—was multifaceted in that it encompassed structured interviews with agency personnel (Phase I developmental survey), reviews of case medical records including utilization information, and evaluation of health outcomes (Phase II). While our primary focus was on the structural components of care, conceptually inherent in our approach as noted in chapter 2 was Donabedian's tripartite schema for the evaluation of the quality of care.[1] Thus, our purpose was to appraise the effectiveness and efficiency of the administrative, financial, and organizational patterns for the delivery of service. However, we clearly recognized the hazards in the use of structure alone as an index of the adequacy of care.

Phase I Developmental-Year Agency Survey

This preliminary phase of the FCHS investigation consisted of an examination of health services to foster children in fourteen voluntary child-care agencies. This developmental effort was undertaken to obtain baseline data that would provide a foundation for subsequent evaluation. The fourteen agencies that participated in the Phase I study represented 10,251 children, or 68 percent of all foster boarding-home children in private placement in New York City ($n = 15,104$) (see table 6-1). They were selected in a purposive manner from the universe of forty-five private facilities that offer care in family or boarding-home placement settings. Selection criteria were size (an attempt was made to select those agencies with the largest family-care case load) and sociodemographic factors (age range of case load, ethnic mix, and religion).

On the advice of the study advisory committee, we excluded from this developmental-study sample those agencies that provided primarily institutional, group-home, and residential treatment services. We also excluded the New York City Bureau of Child Welfare direct-care program that serves about 4,000 charges in a variety of placement settings.

This developmental-study sample included 28 percent white, 49 percent black, and 22 percent Puerto Rican children. These figures reflect well the prevailing characteristic of the New York City population of foster children.[2]

At each of these agencies, site visits were conducted and interviews were held with administrators, medical directors, nurses, psychiatrists, psychologist, dentists, and other professional staff members engaged in the direct delivery or planning of health services. The interviews lasted two to three hours, with total interviewing time per agency ranging from one to two days.

The instrument used for data collection was a questionnaire that consisted of both closed- and open-ended questions focusing on the following dimensions: scope of services—medical, mental health, and dental; staffing patterns; hours of service; nature of the service structure—that is, centralized versus decentralized care; payment mechanisms; and expenditures. In addition, supplementary materials were gathered—for example, statistical cost reports, program descriptions, annual reports, and policy statements.

Several of the specific questions we sought to answer in the interviews with agency personnel were as follows:

What are staff perceptions of the problems of delivering medical care?

Table 6-1
Developmental-Year Agency Characteristics

Agency	Total	Per cent	Ethnic Group								Age								Religion					
			White		Black		Puerto Rican		Other		Under 2		2-5		6-11		12 and over		Catholic		Protestant		Jewish	
			Num-ber	Per-cent	Num-ber	Per-cent	Num-ber	Per-cent	Num-ber	Per-cent	Num-ber	Per-cent	Num-ber	Per-cent	Num-ber	Per-cent	Num-ber	Per-cent	Num-ber	Per-cent	Num-ber	Per-cent	Num-ber	Per-cent
Catholic																								
A	2,158	100	1,131	54	451	21	564	26	12	—	307	14	638	30	728	34	485	22	2,134	99	23	1	1	—
B	1,615	100	517	32	276	17	816	51	6	—	196	12	436	27	551	34	432	27	1,613	99	2	—	0	0
G	630	100	297	47	118	18	189	30	26	4	82	13	124	20	259	41	165	26	619	90	11	2	0	0
K	487	100	188	39	103	21	192	39	4	—	130	27	187	38	152	31	18	4	481	99	6	1	0	0
H	545	100	97	18	116	21	332	61	0	0	72	13	237	43	178	33	58	11	504	92	41	8	0	0
Protestant																								
C	1,188	100	58	5	1,117	94	11	—	2	—	401	34	530	45	245	21	12	1	50	4	1,131	95	7	—
D	684	100	34	5	607	89	39	6	4	—	43	6	186	27	323	47	132	19	17	2	666	97	1	—
F	580	100	31	5	512	88	34	6	3	—	17	3	74	13	262	45	227	39	14	2	566	90	0	0
I	520	100	38	7	482	93	0	0	0	0	64	12	119	23	170	33	167	32	2	—	518	99	0	0
E	487	100	53	11	420	86	11	2	3	—	49	10	84	17	178	37	176	36	3	—	483	99	1	—
L	417	100	29	7	360	86	18	4	10	2	42	10	75	18	174	42	126	30	0	0	417	100	0	0
M	248	100	29	12	215	87	2	—	2	—	53	21	91	37	64	26	40	16	0	0	248	100	0	0
Jewish																								
J	498	100	390	78	92	18	13	3	3	—	155	31	145	29	163	33	35	7	3	—	67	13	428	86
N	194	100	28	14	140	72	13	7	13	7	162	84	28	14	163	3	1	—	60	31	97	50	37	19

Source: These figures have been compiled from the population reports submitted by foster-care agencies for children in care on December 31, 1971 (Form M-284, revised September 18, 1968).

What factors adversely affect the quality and delivery of health services in their agencies?

What are the major obstacles to the provision of comprehensive and continuous care?

How readily available are health services to foster children?

What are staff views of the existing structure for providing medical pediatric care?

How does the present distribution of responsibility and authority within the health-care system facilitate or block the delivery of care?

The following analysis of interview responses, for the most part, shall provide descriptive statements of points of commonality among the various programs. In addition, where a particular response was elicited from less than a majority of agencies but was considered substantively noteworthy, it was included in this presentation. Finally, evaluative comments have been appended wherever they were deemed worthwhile.

Philosophy

No single model characterized the agency health-delivery systems. However, two basically contrasting organizational models were uncovered: (1) an emphasis on centralization of health services to ensure control over the adequacy and quality of care and (2) an emphasis on decentralization of medical services, with primary utilization of local practitioners in order to integrate the locus of the child's care with that of the foster family.

The major differences that result from adherence to these disparate approaches are evident in the degree to which particular agencies incorporate in-house and community resources in the provision of these services. For example:

An in-house clinic, usually located at the agency headquarters and staffed by annual, per session, or per hour medical staff, versus private practitioners located in the area of the child's foster home, who may or may not serve on a panel, paid on a fee-for-service basis;

In-house staff specialists versus private specialists, outpatient specialty clinics of voluntary and municipal hospitals, or comprehensive child-care centers;

A dental clinic located at the agency headquarters, staffed by annual per diem or per hour dental staff versus local community dentists, possibly on a panel, paid on a fee-for-service basis;

In-house psychiatric and psychological staff paid on an annual per session or per diem basis versus private psychiatrists and psychologists.

Agency Medical Director

The position of agency medical director is critical to the effective delivery of services. In recognition of this fact, the New York State Department of Social Services requires child-caring agencies to retain a medical director, preferably a pediatrician, to supervise and integrate services.[3] In addition to stipulating that a child-caring agency employ an attending physician or medical director, who shall be "licensed and currently registered to practice medicine in accordance with the Laws of New York State," New York State regulations further state that the "attending physician or medical director of an institution principally caring for babies and children of pre-school age also be a Diplomate of the American Board of Pediatrics."[4] Among the agencies studied, considerable disparity was found with respect to the role of the medical director, his hours of service, and his responsibilities. Eleven of the fourteen agencies employed a medical director with a specialization in pediatrics. Of the other three, two had no medical director and one had a nominal medical director whose primary function is that of chief psychiatrist. In addition, two of the agencies—one described as having a nominal medical director and one with no medical director—had a case load of children more than half of whom were under five years of age. Moreover, in the eleven agencies employing a so-called medical director, hours of service ranged from three a month to forty a week, with the majority of medical directors devoting from three hours a month to six hours a week to agency service. These diverse patterns of medical supervisory time and leadership may very well have an impact on the nature and scope of services provided to the foster-care child. The fact that duties vary in the time required to complete them and that they must be rendered at the agency suggests that the number of hours that most medical directors are presently devoting to agency service may be less than sufficient. Further, functions that are being performed by the director may be less than optimal in view of the time limitations—for instance, the above-mentioned director who is present only three hours per month was criticized by a foster parent as always seeming rushed during routine examinations.

Scope of Services

Comprehensive care connotes the provision of preventive therapeutic and rehabilitative services, offered in a continuous and personalized manner. As a consequence, agencies in the study were asked to indicate the number of functional areas in which services were provided. Here concern focused on the scope of services—that is, whether it was inclusive or limited. Is provision made for preventive, diagnostic, and therapeutic pediatric, medical, dental, psychiatric, and specialty services? What are the varying emphases placed upon these diverse components of care?

Responses here are organized around three principal program components: (1) pediatric services, (2) dental services, and (3) mental-health services.

Pediatric Services.

Past Medical History. Prior to accepting a child for placement, the sampled agencies uniformly attempt to secure all relevant past medical history. In most instances, the caseworker has primary responsibility for securing such information though an agency nurse and/or medical secretary may be involved. In ten of the sampled agencies, respondents remarked that the past medical histories were usually incomplete. This, it was stated, was due frequently to incomplete referral summaries as well as the unavailability of the natural parent as a source of such information. Such gaps in knowledge point to the possibility of duplication of services (for example, provision of unnecessary immunizations) as well as the failure to detect nonmanifest health problems.

The impression gained by the study team was that agencies differ in the degree to which their casework staff attempts to uncover past health information. This, in turn, may be related to the often-cited comment that casework staff tend to underemphasize the significance of physical-health aspects of a foster child's care—a problem that requires increased in-service training of caseworkers with regard to the importance of health concerns.

Initial Physical Examination. In almost all these agencies, children have their first evaluation prior to placement with the family. In the remaining agencies, initial examinations may be provided at the time of, or just after, placement, especially in the event of an emergency admission.

Except in those instances when a child is accepted in an emergency and there is no time for the administration of formal procedures prior to placement, the initial physical examination should be provided prior to placement and the results of the examination made available to the prospective foster parent. This is especially critical where the child's past medical history indicates the existence or possibility of health problems that might affect the parents' decision to accept the child.

Routine Medical Services. The structure of each agency's medical program for routine, acute, and specialty services does not always relate to the extent of the agency's responsibility to the children under its auspices. More than half of the sampled agencies require that foster children receive routine health care at a centrally located headquarters clinic. Several of the agencies provide transportation through the use of agency cars and/or an escort service, but the majority encourages the foster mother to use her own car, public transportation, or cab, if necessary. In nine of the fourteen agencies studied, routine physical examinations are rendered by the medical director and/or staff physicians. No uniform pattern emerged with respect to clinic staffing among the agencies. Three staff pediatricians, five R.N.s and three secretaries provide routine care and follow-up service to 507 children in one agency, while in another agency only two L.P.N.s are available to assist the director in the provision of preventive care for a comparable number of charges. The professionals usually are assisted by an R.N. and occasionally by the child's caseworker. In three of the other agencies, routine care is given by a panel physician and, in the last agency, by the foster mother's choice of local physician.

Schedules for clinic sessions vary markedly and range from daily clinics, 9 A.M.–5 P.M., to single morning or afternoon clinics, to the absence of any headquarters clinic sessions. Seven of the agencies use an appointment system.

The required minimum schedule for provision of preventive health care by age category (at the time of this study), as promulgated by the New York State Department of Social Services, is as follows:

Age of Child	Frequency of Examination
Zero to six months	Monthly
Six months to one year	Bimonthly
One year to six years	Semi-annually
Seven years and older	Annually

At the end of six years, a child under this schedule would have received nineteen routine physical examinations. Ten of the sampled agencies adhere to this schedule. The four other agencies meet the requirements only for particular age categories: One provides eighteen routine examinations in the six-year period, two provide fifteen examinations, and one provides only twelve. Although several facilities reported that they perform more than the required number of examinations for certain age groups, they fall short of the New York State requirements.

Acute Illness and Emergency Care. The agencies uniformly encourage foster parents to utilize a local or family practitioner or the outpatient department of a local hospital for acute care and emergencies. If the illness is not emergent and occurs during working hours, the foster mother usually is instructed to contact her caseworker or the agency nurse prior to enlisting treatment services. Follow-up is the responsibility of the nurse, caseworker, or medical director.

Specialized Medical Services. Agencies utilize outpatient clinics of local voluntary or municipal hospitals and private practitioners for most specialized medical services. Less often used are comprehensive child-care centers. Specialty resources are selected most commonly through the use of state and local medical directories or on the basis of the recommendation of the medical director or their personal acquaintance with the provider. Concerning staff responsibility for referrals, marked differences emerged, with such duties assigned either to the medical director, staff pediatrician, staff nurse, caseworker, or the local or panel physician.

Dental Services. Decentralized dental services are used by ten of the sample agencies. These resources include the foster families' dentists, local dentists, a panel or quasi-panel of practitioners, or a combination of these. Centralized dental care is provided in the other agencies by staff, panel dentists, or through a headquarters clinic staffed by per session dentists and assistants.

More than half of the fourteen agencies reported that routine dental care is provided on a semi-annual basis. The rest stipulate an annual examination, the minimum New York State requirement. In all but one of the agencies the examinations are scheduled to begin at three years of age. The methods used to ensure follow-up and continuity of dental care are markedly varied, appearing particularly lax in agencies without in-house dental staff to supervise and monitor the care rendered in the community. Three of the most common methods of follow-up reported are utilizing the dentist's bill as an indication of continuing treatment, keeping a record of ongoing reports, and requiring that the caseworker or field nurse have ongoing communication with the foster parent. The individuals most often cited as responsible for coordination and follow-up are the secretary (in-house) and/or the caseworker (field visits).

In general, agency dental programs lacked a readily available and qualified staff, procedures for monitoring dental care, dental-health educational materials, and formal written guidelines. The relative underemphasis of dental care corroborates the findings in several interviews conducted with foster parents, which revealed an ignorance and/or lack of concern with dental health.

Mental-Health Services. Psychiatric services in the sample facilities are rendered principally by in-house part-time or full-time staff psychiatrists or consultants (one agency employs two full-time and ten part-time psychiatrists). In nine agencies, in-house staff is supplemented by community resources. The remaining five facilities rarely or never utilize community mental-health resources. Agencies differ with respect to the type of professional they retain to direct the mental-health program. In seven agencies a child psychiatrist is employed; one agency's chief psychologist serves in this capacity; two agencies employ a consultant psychiatrist; two agencies use administrative (nonmedical) personnel to direct the program; and two agencies have no one person functioning in this capacity.

Psychological services in most of the agencies are rendered by a staff ranging from one to six full-time and/or part-time professionals. Community psychological resources are utilized rarely. Usually, staff psychologists are involved in diagnostic testing and interviewing, though they may provide some in-service training of caseworkers. In all the agencies the primary staff source of referrals is the caseworker; the school (indirectly, through the caseworker) is the primary community source of referral. While diagnostic testing is not a routine procedure at intake, several agencies screen for mental-health problems at regular age intervals—for example, at the start of or at graduation from elementary school, junior high, and/or high school.

In-house staff hours devoted to mental-health services range from 22 hours per week to 143 hours per week among the agencies studied. Also significant is the disparity in the number of children receiving treatment, ranging from 6 (under 2 percent) in an agency with 225 charges to 350 (almost 18 percent) in an agency with 2,136 charges. Treatment may consist of either individual therapy by a psychiatrist or group therapy or counseling by a caseworker under the supervision of a staff psychiatrist.

Standard for the Provision of Care

Explicit formulation of criteria and specificity in standards is the optimum way to assure uniformity as well as to evaluate care. Here we were interested in the degree to which such standards are formalized (that is, in writing) and made operational. According to what criteria are foster children seen routinely for medical and dental preventive care? Are there recommended or required procedures for the foster mother to follow in the event of an acute illness, emergency, or hospitalization?

The majority of agencies reported that they utilize written guidelines for health care—most frequently, those promulgated by the American Board of Pediatrics.[5] Additional sources of health-care standards cited included those set forth by the Child Welfare League of America and in-house guidelines prepared by agency medical directors.[6] The frequency of revision of guidelines varies depending upon the source. In some instances, the revision of in-house guidelines is the sole responsibility of the medical director; in other instances, the directors of each service—medical, dental, mental health—have the responsibility for modification of their respective sections.

With regard to these findings, it should be noted that not one of the fourteen sampled agencies mentioned utilization of the guidelines required by the New York State Department of Social Services; that of those guidelines mentioned, not one was used uniformly by all agencies; that guidelines adopted by the various agencies differ in content, scope, and specificity; that the degree to which guidelines are made available—for example, in an agency manual—to relevant agency staff, panel or local physicians, and/or foster parents, varies; and that the strictness of adherence to guidelines varies from one agency to another.

With regard to dental care, it was found that standards and guidelines were left to the discretion of the individual dentist providing care.

Medical Records

The quality, continuity, and comprehensiveness of care are contributed to by the quality of the medical records that provide evidence of the child's needs and the agency's response to those needs. Our study was concerned with the degree to which all pertinent health information was recorded in a centralized medical record. It was further concerned with how agencies organize and maintain treatment reports including entering diagnoses and follow-up visits.

Although each agency reported that a centralized medical record is maintained for each child in care, there are marked differences in the comprehensiveness, coherence, and completeness of these records. Usually, the record comprises the child's past medical history, developmental history, and immunization and illness reports. The health histories of the natural family and/or the foster family are usually included in the casework file, not in the medical record. Mental-health information, moreover, in several agencies is kept in a separate file, as is the child's dental record.

Monitoring and Review

A critical aspect of agency service is the ability to monitor and review care directly provided or purchased by the agency for the child. It is assumed that any practical and rational system of health care should have some means to determine the acceptability and effectiveness of the professionals utilized. Among the agencies sampled, the criterion for utilization of a local physician was sometimes little more than the recommendation of the foster mother; neither was the medical director always involved in the selection process nor were onsite office visits undertaken. Although all treatment, laboratory, and X-ray reports should be reviewed by a medically trained person to assure effective treatment and follow-up, this is not always the prevailing practice. The results further revealed that periodic, systematic self-appraisals to evaluate the quality, availability, and continuity of medical services rendered are not an integral part of these medical programs.

The following comments, which represent the perceptions of agency staff, are presented in categories that reflect the assumptions that underlie optimum pediatric foster-care services.

Availability and Accessibility of Services

Acceptable and accessible pediatric, specialist, and mental-health professionals are difficult to retain in outlying areas of Long Island as well as upstate New York. Consequently, the service needs of a particular child may require that he/she travel into Manhattan for care. The sources of care utilized—that is, panel pediatricians, specialists, dentists, mental-health professionals, and clinics—are not always located within a reasonable distance from the home of the foster family.

Although rapid transportation is available along lines radiating from the central city, transportation connecting these radial lines to outlying areas is much slower, requiring the use of one or more connecting bus lines or private automobiles.

The formulation and utilization of lists of qualified professionals in outlying areas, it was noted, would facilitate the provision of prompt, appropriate, and accessible service.

In defense of centralization and in response to increasing pressures to decentralize their delivery systems, several agencies stressed the need for central control over the services rendered. Without such control, it was stated, funds would be expended for care of unknown, highly variable, and possibly poor quality.

The need to augment in-house nursing and medical clerical staff was cited. In one agency, a single registered nurse has primary responsibility, including clerical, for a program encompassing approximately 600 foster children.

Existing psychiatric and psychological staff cannot always effectively meet the needs of those children requiring service. Several agencies cited that resources for foster children with emotional problems are inadequate. The skewed availability of qualified mental-health professionals necessarily confines the number of treatment hours. Here again, a network of approved and available resources would facilitate the referral process, particularly in outlying areas.

A commonly expressed need was for the agencies' incorporation of adolescent clinics.

Coordination, Continuity, Follow-up

Agencies lacking an available and concerned medical director or staff pediatrician are characterized by poor coordination of services and inadequate follow-up of care.

Overall scheduling, coordination, and follow-up of health services are often the responsibility of casework staff, who not only have limited knowledge of the child's medical needs but often consider the medical aspects of care to be ancillary to their primary social-service role. Follow-up, therefore, often depends on individual caseworker concern, experience, aggressiveness, and health sophistication.

Many agencies lack a dental director, consultant, or qualified professional charged with the responsibility of making judgments and monitoring the work performed in this area. In general, dental care is left too much to the discretion of local practitioners, with inadequate agency-centralized control.

Coordination of dental services is variously the responsibility of the nurse, medical secretary, or caseworker. The absence of explicitly defined roles, in some instances, results in minimal follow-up and control over preventive dental and treatment services rendered; a child may be seen for thorough prophylaxis and examination, but subsequent intensive treatments may be haphazard.

Agencies do not routinely evaluate foster children for emotional problems. Hence, there may be children who, if unreferred, remain undiagnosed and untreated. This was reflected in the responses to questions concerning dissatisfaction, many of which made reference to the potentially large number of undiagnosed children in need of mental-health services. Since the caseworker, most commonly, is the primary source of such referrals, the need for more-intensive caseworker training in this area is indicated. Concurrently, more-extensive screening of agency clientele would facilitate detection and follow-up of mental-health problems.

Medical programs that retain in-house mental-health staff rather than community resources have greater control and supervision over the services rendered. In contradistinction, coordination and follow-up is often poor in agencies that utilize primarily decentralized mental-health resources.

Poor communication between medical and psychiatric staff often exists.

Psychiatric follow-up is often poor, with haphazard reporting.

Accountability, Reporting Evaluations

Agencies do not always know the names of local practitioners providing care, and they do not always keep a record of treatment rendered.

Criteria for panel acceptance may be little more than the recommendation of the foster mother; the medical director does not always assist in the selection of panel members; and on-site visits are not undertaken.

Systematic attention to the monitoring and control of care rendered in the community by the local pediatrician, specialist, or dentist is notable by its absence. Agencies that manifested interest in such regulatory activities did so usually because of the presence of an agressive and concerned medical director.

Local pediatric, dental, and mental-health practitioners often were cited as guilty of poor reporting practices—for example, they did not always submit a complete written report along with their claims for payment. Moreover, there is no assurance that reports will be submitted promptly.

Formal, periodic agency self-evaluation of its health program was rare, as was the concomitant availability of complete and accurate utilization statistics.

Phase II Evaluation: Case Medical-Record Reviews and Health Evaluation

This section describes the extent to which the health-care services provided these children have met their basic medical-care needs. The principal research tools for gathering data were medical-record reviews and direct clinical examinations as outlined in this book. Chapter 2 describes these instruments in detail. In brief, the review form provided a profile of each child's medical history and identified the pattern, completeness, and adequacy of preventive, diagnostic, and treatment services. The direct clinical examinations provided data on the physical, psychological, and psychiatric status of the children.

Because communicable diseases of childhood (diphtheria, tetanus, whooping cough, measles, and poliomyelitis) still constitute important potential causes of sickness, pediatric standards recommend that children be protected during the first few months of life with vaccinations and also with booster immunizations given around eighteen months, four to six years, and fourteen to fifteen years.[7] The data from the sample records showed that such procedures were not administered consistently to the study group but that differences on an interagency level were marked (table 6–2). Over half of the preschool children had no record of immunizations against mumps (68 percent), about two-fifths apparently were unprotected against measles (36 percent) and rubella (43 percent), and close to one-fifth had not been fully immunized against polio (19 percent) and diphtheria, tetanus, and pertussis (23 percent).

Sensory screening tests, which are recommended as a routine adjunct to health-supervision visits, also were not regularly performed and recorded for these children. Three-fifths of those between three and fifteen years old who were examined did not have a recorded visual examination for the five-year period preceding the study, more than 90 percent did not have hearing-test information in their charts, and more than half did not have a recorded dental examination in the five-year period. As evident from table 6–3 significant interagency differences existed in this regard.

The performance of laboratory tests for anemia and tuberculosis is an important part of good pediatric care, but two-thirds of the sample did not have a recorded hemoglobin or hematocrit test, and one-fourth did not have tuberculin-test data in their charts for a five-year period. On an interagency level, again we found marked differences for these measures (table 6–3).

Physicians' physical examinations that were evaluated for completeness were found to have been performed and/or recorded inadequately. The nine examination components considered essential for a complete examination were height; weight; ears, nose, and throat; heart; femoral pulses; abdomen; genitalia; extremities; and skin. However, the average number recorded for admission examinations was 6.72 (table 6–4). In addition, for 14 percent of the sample group, no admission examination was recorded. In terms of routine examinations, the component rate was 5.60, with significant differences exhibited on an interagency level.

Related information showed that the source of care for these examinations was not constant. Only 9 percent of the group saw the same doctor for checkups during the five-year period preceding the study, and 61 percent saw two or more different doctors for these examinations. Because a number of different health providers may be involved in the provision of services to each child, an effective referral and follow-up system is essential to ensure optimum care. The health records showed, however, a low overall rate of referrals accomplished—of 363 referrals made over a five-year period, only 216 (59 percent) were accomplished. Again, as may be seen in

Table 6–2
Immunization Levels for Study Children under Six Years of Age as Reported in Medical Records, by Agency

Type of Immunization	Total	Agency							
		One	Two	Three	Four	Five	Six	Seven	Eight
Total percentage	100	100	100	100	100	100	100	100	100
D.P.T.									
None	10	4	2	—	17	5	7	33	13
Less than three	13	11	36	7	3	10	7	16	13
Three or more	77	86	62	93	80	85	86	51	74
Polio									
None	12	4	7	—	14	5	7	33	24
Less than two	7	4	19	—	6	5	2	16	8
Two or more	81	92	74	100	80	90	91	51	68
Measles									
None	36	21	55	27	34	26	16	62	42
One or more	64	79	45	73	66	74	84	38	58
Rubella									
None	43	29	45	32	49	50	27	73	37
One or more	57	71	55	68	51	50	73	27	63
Mumps									
None	68	21	76	88	97	64	39	92	63
One or more	32	79	24	12	3	36	61	8	37

Note: D = Diphtheria, P = Pertussis-whooping cough, T = Tetanus.

Table 6-3
Annual Rates of Dental-, Vision-, and Hearing-Screening and Laboratory Tests for Study Children Three Years or Older, by Agency

Test	Total Children (n = 576)	One (n = 64)	Two (n = 68)	Three (n = 73)	Four (n = 76)	Five (n = 73)	Six (n = 74)	Seven (n = 70)	Eight (n = 78)
						Agency			
Dental	0.43	1.34	0.05	0.35	0.36	0.36	0.27	0.25	0.50
Vision	0.31	0.87	0.63	0.16	0.30	0.19	0.19	0.16	0.11
Hearing	0.05	0.09	0.02	0.07	0.09	0.02	0.07	0.02	—
Tuberculin	0.46	0.89	0.45	0.55	0.55	0.35	0.44	0.20	0.31
Hemoglobin/HCT	0.23	0.35	0.48	0.46	0.02	0.17	0.10	0.25	—
Urinanalysis	0.22	0.81	0.09	0.39	0.05	0.08	0.08	0.21	0.07

Table 6-4
Completeness of Admission Examinations Performed on Study Children, by Agency, as Reported in Medical Records, 1968-1973

Component Recorded	Total[a] (n = 573)	Agency							
		One (n = 78)	Two (n = 80)	Three (n = 81)	Four (n = 76)	Five (n = 91)	Six (n = 63)	Seven (n = 46)	Eight (n = 58)
Total	100	100	100	100	100	100	100	100	100
Height	86	100	70	91	74	99	97	76	72
Weight	92	100	79	98	97	100	97	85	74
HEENT	91	99	88	91	96	100	86	74	86
Heart	85	97	51	90	96	98	81	76	86
Femoral pulses	b	—	1	—	—	—	—	2	—
Abdomen	84	99	56	91	86	97	78	76	86
Genitalia	80	74	62	85	89	98	71	72	53
Extremities	69	95	56	80	72	97	70	46	10
Skin	84	100	64	89	91	95	68	72	83
Admission-examination component rate	6.72	7.64	5.28	7.16	7.01	7.82	6.48	5.78	5.78
Percentage of admission exams with no recorded evidence	14	0	4	6	1	0	26	43	33
Routine examination rate	5.60	4.73	3.30	5.41	7.10	7.66	5.95	3.13	5.45
Number	668	78	83	86	77	91	85	81	87

[a]Number of admission examinations recorded.
[b]Less than 0.5 percent.

table 6-5, agencies varied markedly in the relative emphasis they placed on follow-up.

FCHS data also revealed that a large proportion of children found by study examiners to have health problems had no record of having been seen previously for evaluation or treatment of those problems, but interagency differences were significant (table 6-6).

For the total sample, almost half (47 percent) of those found by clinic examiners to have visual-acuity disorders ($n = 125$) had not been seen by an ophthalmologist or optometrist during the five years preceding the study. More than two-fifths of the children found to be in need of dental treatment had not been seen by a dentist during the same period, and only one-fourth of the children who presented symptoms of emotional or developmental problems ($n = 334$) had been seen for treatment.

Data abstracted from the records also showed that many health problems identified by survey examiners apparently were diagnosed and treated inappropriately or were unknown (or unmentioned in records) to the foster-care agencies. For example, 17 percent of the children found to have poor visual acuity had either inappropriate correction or no correction at all for their problems. Moreover, a high proportion of those tested with their glasses, 61 percent, were found to have inadequate correction. More than 25 percent of those who reportedly wore glasses had normal acuity levels when tested without correction, and 56 percent of those found by survey examiners to have visual problems had no recorded evidence of such a problem in their medical records.

Further data showed that almost all the children classified by survey examiners as abnormal or questionable developmentally had been seen for evaluation of such a problem (98 percent). In addition, nearly all the children who failed the hearing test had no medical record of such a condition (93 percent). Similarly, of the youngsters who exhibited orthopedic problems, psychiatric impairment, or speech disorders at the time of the clinical evaluation, only a small percentage (31 percent, 34 percent, 46 percent respectively) had data in their charts suggesting that these conditions had been diagnosed or treated.

Summary

Both the Phase I agency survey and the Phase II evaluative record study yielded data that clearly suggest deficiencies in the level of care provided to the study's urban foster-care group. Moreover, they indicate that the availability of Medicaid funds does not assure that these children obtain the services they need to stay well. Thus, in terms of outcome data, the essential findings showed that preschoolers had inadequate levels of immunization,

Table 6-5
Number of Referrals Recommended and Accomplished by Physician, by Agency, Based on Data Reported in Medical Records, 1968-1973

						Agency			
Referrals	Total	One	Two	Three	Four	Five	Six	Seven	Eight
Recommended	0.11	0.09	0.16	0.23	0.16	0.04	0.07	0.09	0.05
Accomplished	0.07	0.07	0.10	0.21	0.06	0.02	0.03	0.05	0.01
Ratio accomplished to recommended	0.61	0.84	0.66	0.89	0.36	0.54	0.39	0.58	0.19

Note: Rates are based on the sum of findings in all examinations of the actual number of preventive examinations conducted. The ratios of referrals accomplished to referrals recommended are based on actual referral figures.

Table 6–6
Study Children Found in Need of Dental Treatment and Psychiatric/Psychological Care in Survey Examination as Compared to Visits Recorded in Medical Records, by Agency

					Agency				
	Total	One	Two	Three	Four	Five	Six	Seven	Eight
Dental Care									
Total number in need of dental treatment	179	17	25	31	11	25	27	25	18
Average annual number of dental visits recorded	0.51	1.87	0.02	0.36	1.04	0.35	0.52	.18	0.57
WTD SUM	91	32		11	11	9	14	5	9
STD DEV	.785	.869	.080	.343	1.472	.405	.67	.257	.753
SE MEAN	.059	.211	.016	.062	.444	.081	.150	.069	.177
Psychiatric/Psychological Care									
Total number in need of psychiatric/psychological care	125	27	NA	24	NA	18	NA	31	25
Average annual number of psychiatric/psychological visits recorded	1.24	4.46	NA	0.01	NA	0.01	NA	1.07	0.05
WTD SUM	155	121	NA		NA		NA	33	1
STD DEV	4.750	8.448		.041		.047		4.324	.202
SE MEAN	.425	1.626		.008		.011		.0777	.040

NA = Not available.
WTD SUM = Weighted sum
STD DEV = Standard deviation.
SE MEAN = Standard error of the mean.

that simple laboratory and sensory screening tests were not performed and recorded routinely, that preventive examinations were often incomplete, that referral and follow-up care were frequently haphazard, and that many health problems identified by survey examiners apparently were diagnosed and treated inappropriately or unknown to the foster-care agencies. It is, of course, possible that the sample children indeed were screened, diagnosed, evaluated, and treated but that the information was not recorded in the charts. If that is the case, however, it also represents unacceptable medical care. Adequate care by any standards cannot be provided without maintaining complete and up-to-date medical records. Finally, if effective care is to become a reality, then criteria such as the following must be met:

Setting standards and translating these standards into guidelines for bringing about the accessibility, availability, and acceptability that should be a part of health care;

Developing and implementing written health programs that specify agency policies and procedures with regard to prevention, screening, evaluation, management, and follow-up;

Instituting staff orientation and in-service training to ensure that the objectives of the health program are understood and accepted by all agency personnel including part-time professionals and community providers;

Developing a standard medical-record system that will facilitate the consistent recording of information in a uniform and accurate manner, as well as periodic review of charts to assure that they are kept current;

Establishing a system for coordinating services so children with questionable findings are followed up and evaluated consistently;

Reviewing program objectives periodically to appraise staff performance and to assess the need for change and modification;

Encouraging foster-parent involvement through regular meetings that provide health education and counseling.

Since the children who participated in this study were found to be less healthy than a random sample of comparably aged children drawn from more widely based study groups, it is likely that they are in need of more health care than most children. Unfortunately, our data documented the apparent failure of existing delivery systems to manage effectively even simple and common child health problems. These findings are in accord with a recent Baltimore study of health services for foster children.[8] That study demonstrated that foster children were not only low utilizers of health-care services but also the recipients of inadequate health supervision. In light of these findings, we hope that existing child-welfare facilities will reassess the effectiveness of their health programs. The steps recommended, together with an ongoing emphasis on feedback, quality control, and monitoring activities—that is, professional review of reports to assure appropriate service and case accountability—will serve to generate a balanced and cost-effective system of care that is flexible and responsive to the needs of these children.

Notes

1. Avedis Donabedian, "The Evaluation of Medical Care Programs," *Bulletin of the New York Academy of Medicine* 44, no. 2 (February 1968): 117–124.

2. New York City Department of Social Service, "Summary Analysis of Monthly Population Reports Submitted by Foster Care Agencies," mimeographed (New York, June 30, 1972).

3. New York State Department of Social Services, *Rules and Recommendations for Child Caring Institutions,* pub. no. 1064 (Albany, New York, May 1969).

4. American Academy of Pediatrics, *Standards of Child Health Care,* 3rd ed. (Evanston, Ill., 1977)

5. Ibid.

6. *CWLA Standards for Foster Family Service,* rev. ed. (New York: Child Welfare League of America, 1975).

7. American Academy of Pediatrics, *Standards of Child Health Care.*

8. Edward L. Schor, "The Foster Care System and Health Status of Foster Children," *Pediatrics* 69 (May 1982).

7 Foster-Child Health Status, Utilization of Services, and Evaluation of Care as Reported by Foster Mothers

Though attitudes and satisfactions with health care are difficult to ascertain, the reactions of consumers of care toward a service represents an important measure of system effectiveness. In the field of child welfare, foster parents stand at the juncture between social-agency administrative procedural concerns and the delivery of services. Thus, foster parents are in effect both quasi-consumers and surrogate parents, as well as members of the service team. As such, they play a vital role in the delivery of health care to their charges and offer a viable means of appraising the effectiveness of services rendered.

The data in this book concerning foster children and their health care were gathered through interviews conducted personally with a sample of foster mothers. These interviews had a twofold purpose: (1) to obtain data about foster-child health status and utilization of services as perceived by foster mothers that would serve as a substantive supplement to the agency and health-examination surveys (chapters 4 and 6) and (2) to ascertain the efficiency and effectiveness of health programs as experienced and perceived at the foster-parent level.

The interest in this population stems in part from the increasing significance of consumer advocacies in the evaluation and delivery of health care.[1] Implicit in this move toward consumerism is the view that the recipients of service are entitled to an important voice in how that service is dispensed because who, other than the ultimate users, it is asked, are the proper judges of the kinds of services they want and how they want them delivered?[2] Improvement in the delivery of care demands an involvement and dialogue between the provider and consumer because only the recipient can provide a means of identifying the sensitive and relevant problems not readily perceived by the professional.[3]

Concern with foster parents (as health-service recipients) also derives from the notion that parental attitudes and behavior are related to child-health behavior patterns, that such patterns are acquired within the family, and that a child's ability to recognize symptoms is learned from family members, especially the mother.[4] In this regard, a number of studies in this

area have emphasized the pivotal part the woman plays as the prime orga-
nizer of family health-related activities.[5] For instance, the health responses
of women involve not only home nursing care, and the administration of
medications and escort service but also their role as the principal health
educators and decision makers for their family.[6] Consequently, their attitudes toward health and the degree to which they utilize services to a great
extent influences the attitudes and behavior of other members of their family. Thus, if the mother can be helped to use health services in more-appro-
priate ways, then she can function as a teaching agent through which her
child can develop his or her model for the appropriate use of these services.[7]

While the research in this area has not been extensive, taken together,
the findings usually imply a potential interplay between the foster parents'
health knowledge and practices and the child's attitudes and health behavior and supports the contention that along with agency programs, the
foster parents have great relevance for the health-service utilization of their
charges.[8]

Foster-Family Background Characteristics

The interview population consisted of a subgroup of 256 mothers of
children participating in the health-examination component of the survey,
which as noted earlier, was conducted at the New York Hospital pediatric
outpatient evaluation clinic. The total study group consisted of 668 children
and their foster mothers.

Background data drawn from agency social records revealed that 61
percent of the foster mothers were black and other races, 23 percent were
white, and 12 percent were Puerto Rican. This is a higher proportion of
blacks and Hispanics than for the city as a whole and compares equally well
with the demographic characteristics of all children in New York City foster
homes (see chapter 5). Racial data were unavailable for 11 percent of the
foster fathers, but the overall picture is consistent with that of the foster
mothers. A similar racial profile for the study children suggests a high level
of ethnic homogeneity (18 percent white, 64 percent black, 18 percent
Puerto Rican).

Concerning religious affiliation, half of the foster mothers were Protestant, 40 percent were Catholic and 7 percent were Jewish. The percentage
distributions for the foster fathers, the children, the foster mothers, and the
citywide foster-care population are in close agreement.

Data on educational levels were available for 564 mothers (85 percent
of the sample). Among the group for whom information was available, 24
percent were high school graduates and 22 percent had had only a grammar
school education or less. About one in twenty had had some college, and

1 percent were reported to be college graduates. The educational profile of the foster fathers, to the extent known, roughly parallels that of the foster mothers.

The socioeconomic picture that emerges conforms to expectations. Earnings from the employment of either the foster mother, the foster father, or both provided the main source of income for almost all the study families (82 percent), with a minority receiving public assistance. Most of these families earned less than $10,000 and most of the fathers were engaged in skilled, semiskilled, or unskilled kinds of manual work in the blue-collar range—for example, machine operator, custodian, construction worker. These data are consistent with findings from other studies that characterize foster parents as almost uniformly low on the socioeconomic-status ladder.[9] Related characteristics for this group reveal that they tend to be more traditional, religious, and lower in educational status than the general adult population, all of which may well impact on their health orientation and behavior. In this regard, studies of health and socioeconomic status have reported that attitudes and the manner in which health systems are perceived and interpreted are subject to considerable variation; that is, differentials in educational attainment, purchasing power, social-class life-styles, geographic location, and knowledge of and experience with the medical-care process each contributes to the variability in medical orientations. For example, Wade, in her study of public knowledge about health and illness, found that education is the single most significant predictor variable in establishing the level of health knowledge because it indicates the probability that a person will seek out information.[10]

In other surveys, the level of health and the quality of personal behavior have been shown to be related to socioeconomic status.[11] Koos demonstrated the interrelationship and interaction of a composite of sociodemographic and cognitive factors: the lower the social class and the income, the lower the perception of symptoms needing care and the lower the utilization of health resources.[12] Irelan, after reviewing many similar studies, concluded that in almost every dimension of health care, lower-class behavior is different from middle- and upper-class behavior. The lower class defines health and illness differently, has less-adequate health information, is less inclined to take preventive measures and delays longer in seeking health care.[13] Such behavior is reflected in fewer preventive medical visits for this group (for example, pre- and postnatal care, general checkups), fewer preventive dental visits, a higher percentage of unimmunized children, and lower participation in free immunization programs.[14]

Concerning the sociopsychologic concomitants of the use of health services, research has been neither systematic nor extensive. In one particularly significant study, the author examined medical behavior within the broad framework of a sociocultural setting. Highly skeptical persons (that is, persons who delay in seeking a physician), he found, tended to have less factual knowledge about the medical-care complex and, therefore, utilized its services less often.[15] This finding is similar to those of Anderson and Glasser, both of whom report that utilization of health services varies directly with amount of knowledge held by the patient.[16]

Interview Sample

Each of the 256 mother interviewees received a description of the purpose of the interview and was told that participation was voluntary. None of the mothers approached refused to cooperate, but since the agencies assisted the research team in ensuring parent involvement, many respondents may have felt some pressure or obligation to provide suitable answers. Therefore, some caution must be exercised in the consideration of these results.

The interviews were conducted by three female staff members representing different ethnic groups so as to try to match interviewers and respondents for ethnicity in order to minimize bias in this area. The questionnaire required about sixty minutes for completion. Questions asked of the respondents concerned their foster child's health, the availability and accessibility of services, their knowledge of and experience with agency health programs, and their satisfaction with the agency health-delivery systems. Interviewees were frequently unable to answer every question because of lack of comprehension or of recall, and this is reflected in the total responses tabulated. It also should be kept in mind that this is a sample of New York City foster mothers and foster children at one point in time and is, therefore, weighted in favor of those in long-term foster-care placement situations.

Data on the living arrangements and household composition of the interviewees show that the typical respondent lived in a private three-bedroom house that contained four to six persons (table 7-1). Most of the mothers interviewed (85 percent) had had some experience as biological parents either prior to or during the time they cared for foster children (table 7-2). Relative to their experience as foster parents, one out of three interviewees reported that they had cared for foster children for six to ten years, and another one-fourth replied that they had been a foster mother for one to five years. When interviewed, the majority of respondents was caring for more than one foster child (85 percent). Of these, half cared for two or three children, and only a minority had four or more charges.

Although most respondents had more than one foster child in their home at the time of the interview, the information gathered was limited to the child that participated in the health-examination component of this study. As a group, these children ranged in age from one to fifteen years,

Table 7–1

Foster-Mother Living Accommodations and Household Size

Living Accommodations	Total	
	Number	Percent
Total interview sample	256	100
Type of accommodations		
Private house	194	76
Apartment house	38	15
Project	23	9
No answer	1	a
Number of people in dwelling unit		
Under 4	78	30
4–6	166	65
7–9	61	24
10 or more	4	1
No answer	1	a
Total number of rooms per dwelling unit		
3	1	a
4–5	65	25
6–7	84	33
8–9	51	20
10 or more	25	10
No answer	30	12
Number of bedrooms per dwelling unit		
1	2	1
2	39	15
3	116	45
4–5	89	35
6–7	9	4
No answer	1	a

[a] Less than 0.5 percent.

with 84 percent between one and eleven years (table 7–3). The range for length of placement was from six months to over six years. Children in placement more than two years were considered long-term placements (two out of three); all others were classified as short-term.

Results

The following data present the respondents' knowledge and attitudes as they relate to the health status and health utilization of the study children.

Table 7–2
Foster Mothers' Experience in Caring for Foster Children and Natural Children

Care Experience	Total	
	Number	Percent
Total	256	100
Number whose study child is first and only foster child	50	20
Number who have cared for other foster children	206	80
Length of time caring for all		
More than ten years	45	17
Six–ten years	85	33
One–five years	69	27
Less than one year	3	1
No answer	4	2
Number of foster children presently in care		
Study child only	38	15
Two	90	35
Three	40	15
Four or more	36	14
No answer	2	1
Number of foster mothers with natural children	217	85
Number of natural children		
One	52	20
Two	63	25
Three	56	22
Four or more	46	18
Number of foster mothers with natural child under eighteen living at home	139	54
Number of foster mothers with no child under eighteen living at home	82	31
Number of foster mothers with no natural children	39	15

The questions focus on the mother's perception of the child's past and present health, the child's symptomatology during recent months, and the child's use of medical services. In addition, the perceptions and observations regarding agency medical practices and the availability of services are

Table 7–3

Age of Foster Child at Time of Foster-Mother Interview and Number of Years in This Placement

Age and Length of Time in Placement	Total	
	Number	Percent
Total	256	100
Under six years of age	117	46
One	13	5
Two	14	6
Three	28	11
Four	29	11
Five	33	13
Six to eleven years of age	98	38
Six	23	9
Seven	18	7
Eight	16	6
Nine	16	6
Ten	14	6
Eleven	11	4
Twelve years and over	41	16
Twelve	19	7
Thirteen	22	9
Number of years in this placement		
Less than one year	19	8
One	39	15
Two	38	15
Three	44	17
Four	26	10
Five	16	6
Six or more	74	29

explored through a series of questions that focus on areas such as what, if any, medical advice and health information have been formalized (that is, put in writing) and made operational and when and how services could or should be obtained for their foster-care charges.

Foster-Child Health Status and Utilization of Services

Over one-third of the mothers, 37 percent, described their foster child's health as fair or poor at the time of placement, 50 percent rated the child's health as good, and an additional 13 percent called it excellent. By contrast, almost all of the respondents, 94 percent, evaluated the study child's present health as either excellent or good. A comparison of the health of these children with that of a welfare sample and a national sample shows that over a third of the welfare mothers regarded their child's health as fair or poor compared to only 3 percent of the national sample and 6 percent of our foster-care group.[17]

Whether these differences are attributable in whole or in part to real differences in objective health-status or to differences in the perceptions of the natural mothers and foster mothers can be determined only by an examination of FCHS direct physical-examination data. Such an evaluation indicates that the foster mothers in this survey, viewed against the findings of the study pediatricians, hold an overly positive view of their children's health. Thus, as described in chapter 5, the children in this survey, upon examination, were found to be less healthy than comparably aged children drawn from more widely based groups, but their health status and medical care needs were at levels roughly comparable to that of other low-income and minority-group populations; 37 percent had health problems requiring referral for specialty care, almost half had chronic medical problems, and 35 percent of those evaluated by survey psychiatrists exhibited marked to severe levels of emotional impairment.

The responses of the interviewees to a somewhat different measure of health were more consistent with the opinions of the survey pediatricians. When asked whether they were bothered or worried about their study child's physical or emotional health, 44 percent replied in the affirmative. In contrast, a nationwide survey found that only 17 percent of a representative sample of parents had concerns or worries about some aspect of their child's health.[18] The mothers in this study also reported that behavioral and/or emotional problems were the principal cause of their concern. Thus, one out of five respondents (21 percent) said their child had a behavioral problem, and one in three (33 percent) reported that the child had seen a mental-health professional during the study year or prior to that time for such a problem. However, 12 percent felt that their study child needed care in this area that had not been provided.

Visits to a doctor for preventive or therapeutic reasons were also ascertained, revealing that during the study year, there were an average of 4 visits per child, which is fewer than the figure obtained from agency medical records. The record data indicated 5.37 visits for preschool and 4.24 visits for school-age members of our sample. Figures from the 1975 national health interview survey reveal that children under five years had approximately 5.3 visits per year, whereas the figure for those between five and fourteen years was 2.9 visits per year.[19] Since our sample exhibited higher rates of disability and illness than the U.S. general child population, it is possible that they would have more-frequent medical contacts than the children in the Health Interview Survey.[20] However, medical-care events like the utilization of services are influenced by a variety of factors that affect the reliability of the data—for example, the scheduling of preventive-care visits, the mothers' knowledge and awareness of medical practices, the availability and accessibility of services, and the financial arrangements or medical coverage. In regard to the latter, a number of studies have shown that the utilization of health services by low-income children like those in our sample has increased since the inception of Medicaid. In fact, some surveys suggest that poor children supported by Medicaid today have almost equal levels of utilization as the nonpoor.[21] For example, in a Michigan study that examined the impact of Medicaid on the use of ambulatory services, Medicaid children averaged 2.44 visits per year for illness-related conditions as compared with 1.97 visits for the non-Medicaid group.[22] In addition, the study reported that by 1977, children covered by Medicaid were seeing more doctors for preventive as well as acute-care reasons than those not covered by Medicaid. Moreover, further analysis revealed that the children in the low-income group who were covered by Medicaid had a greater number of preventive checkups, acute-illness visits, as well as total visits to physicians than those low-income children not financed by Medicaid.

Despite these changes in doctor utilization for low-income children, national and local studies indicate that removing the financial obstacles to care has not increased the use of private practitioners. Thus, available data show that a two-tier system remains, with Medicaid children less likely to use a pediatrician and to have a usual source of care and far more likely to use public-sector providers for their medical care, such as outpatient clinics of hospitals, emergency rooms, and health centers, than other more-advantaged children.[23] Thus, a Rhode Island survey found that nine out of ten non-Medicaid low-income persons had a private doctor compared with two out of three of the Medicaid poor.[24] Moreover, 1974 national data show that 63 percent of Medicaid poor children (income of $5,000 or less) had a private physician or group-practice provider as their regular source of care as against approximately nine out of ten upper-income children (income of $15,000 or more).[25]

How does our Medicaid-financed urban sample of foster children fit into this picture? What are their utilization patterns? As may be seen in table 7-4, 43 percent of the mothers reported that the agency headquarters clinic provided routine service for their foster children. Another 28 percent said that the children usually were seen for checkups in the office of a private doctor selected by the agency, and 11 percent replied that they utilized a local doctor whom they had selected. That less reliance is placed on clinic utilization for preventive care is reflected by the fact that only 9 percent of the mothers responding to this item reported the use of self-selected hospital clinics and 8 percent agency-assigned clinics.

A corresponding question asked if the foster child usually saw the same

Table 7-4
Source of Preventive Health Care for Study Children as Reported by Foster Mother

Source of Care	Number	Percent
Total sample	256	100
Private doctor	99	39
(Agency selected)		(28)
(Foster mother selected)		(11)
Agency medical clinic	111	43
Hospital outpatient clinic	42	17
Other	1	a
Never had checkup	3	1

a Less than 0.5 percent.

doctor for preventive health checkups. Sixty-five percent said all the time and 10 percent responded never. (Ten percent did not know or did not answer, and three mothers said their foster child never went for checkups.) In addition, when asked if the doctor seen was a pediatrician, 65 percent replied affirmatively, 15 percent replied negatively, but 5 percent did not know what kind of doctor the child saw and 14 percent did not respond to this item. For 70 percent of the respondents the provider was located less than thirty minutes away, for 15 percent the time was between thirty minutes and one hour, and for 14 percent the doctor was one hour or more away. Sixteen percent of the mothers felt that the location of this provider was inconvenient. In terms of waiting times for treatment, 40 percent said the wait was thirty minutes or less, 15 percent reported one hour, and 9 percent said two hours or more. Fourteen percent did not respond to this item. When the mothers were asked about satisfaction with care on the child's last preventive health visit, three out of four replied they were very satisfied and one out of ten expressed dissatisfaction. The remainder did not respond to this item.

Respondent replies to a series of questions dealing with acute-care services revealed that 30 percent of these children use the same doctor for checkups that they use for acute illnesses, but more than half (56 percent) use a different doctor for these services. For one-fourth of the mothers using a separate acute-care provider, the agency assigns this private practitioner, and for another one-third the doctor is self-selected. In addition, self-selected clinics were said to be the source of acute-care services for 26 percent of this group, and agency-assigned clinics were the source for another 16 percent.

The mothers also were asked if their foster children usually see the same doctor at each acute-illness visit. Over half (52 percent) replied all of the time, 8 percent said most of the time, 5 percent reported some of the time, and 22 percent responded never. When asked if the doctor seen was a pediatrician, 52 percent said yes, 22 percent said no, and 26 percent either did not know or did not respond to this item. For 71 percent, travel time was less than thirty minutes, for 4 percent it was between thirty minutes and one hour, and for 2 percent it was one hour or more. Twenty percent did not answer this item. In terms of waiting times, 42 percent reported that they waited twenty-five minutes or less to see this doctor in his office, and 19 percent replied that they waited one hour or more.

Fourteen percent of the foster mothers said that the study child was receiving specialty care regularly, and half indicated that a social/emotional/behavioral problem was being treated. When asked about the source of care for this specialty service, 44 percent reported that the service was provided at a hospital clinic, 24 percent said the agency headquarters clinic, and 32 percent indicated that a private physician provided the treatment. When asked if their child saw the same provider for each visit, 58 percent replied all of the time, 2 percent said some of the time, 11 percent reported never, and the remainder either did not respond or said they did not know.

In terms of dental care, 85 percent of the respondents reported that their study child had visited a dentist within the twelve months preceding the interview, with the service provided primarily by private dentists rather than public providers. This is a far greater level of dental utilization than reported for other pediatric populations. For example, a 1977 Michigan survey documented that 48 percent of low-income children covered by Medicaid had not been to the dentist in the last year compared with 27 percent of a non-Medicaid sample. Moreover, among those without Medicaid support, 47 percent had not visited a dentist, suggesting that removing financial barriers did not lead to greater dental utilization for the poor children in that community.[26] Available national data show that half of the children under fifteen and more than half of those in low-income areas had never been to a dentist, compared with 11 percent from our interview sample.[27]

While it is not possible to say whether these differences are attributable to differences in the use of services or to differences in the perceptions of respondents, a comparison with data from our dental-screening tests and record survey would seem to suggest that these foster mothers hold a favorable view of their child's dental health and use of services.

Thus, figures from the FCHS medical-record survey revealed that on the average, for the period 1968–1973, 38 out of 100 sample children had one visit to a dentist per year. Moreover, the level of utilization showed a positive association with foster-parent occupational strata and income, with children in homes where the annual income was higher and where the foster father was an administrator or skilled worker having more dental visits than other children. In addition, although only one out of ten foster mothers said their foster child had unmet dental needs, data from the FCHS health-examination survey (as reported in chapter 3) indicated that over half of the children examined had one or more decayed teeth, with the level of decay rising sharply and consistently with age. An earlier study of school-age indigent children in Chicago produced the strikingly high decay rate of 97 percent,[28] while between 40 and 90 percent of preschool Head Start children were found to have dental caries.[29] By contrast, evidence from the broad-based Health Examination Survey (HES) investigation revealed that one in four children between six and eleven years and one in two children between twelve and seventeen had one or more decayed teeth.[30]

These comparisons seem to suggest that the dental needs of FCHS children are at levels comparable to those of other disadvantaged groups and significantly greater than the levels of more socially and economically representative samples. Further, this widespread prevalence of dental decay seems to indicate that dental care has been provided neither promptly, consistently, nor adequately in contradistinction to the reports of the sample foster mothers.

Foster-Mother Evaluation of Agency Health Programs

Respondents in this study also were asked to evaluate agency programs through a series of structured questions relating to the quality of care, its comprehensiveness, and the personal manner in which it was given. While an examination of replies revealed an overall satisfaction with the services provided to the sample children, the responses highlighted several areas of concern, outlined in the following sections.

Agency Orientation and Education of Foster Parents. Parent education in preventive health and the emotional and social needs of children should be a vital concern in the administration of any health program. Among foster parents, this is particularly meaningful in view of the neglected and often troubled children that come into their care as well as because these families are often of marginal socioeconomic status with concomitant limited education, particularly in the area of health (for example, study data revealed that the need for adequate dental care is not always fully appreciated and that foster parents occasionally are remiss in meeting scheduled medical appointments and/or ensuring that their children take medications as prescribed).

When the foster mothers in this study were queried about agency orientation and educational activities, there was the occasional comment by a respondent that she had increased her knowledge of child health and was applying this understanding in the medical supervision of her own children. However, when asked specifically about the receipt of information from the social agencies, more than half the mothers claimed that they had not received educational materials (for example, concerning things such as first aid, home safety, proper nutrition, the treatment of common illnesses, or basic pediatric guidelines outlining immunization and preventive health schedules for children of all ages) or appeared to find them unimportant, if received. If, in fact, the agencies do disseminate such materials, it would seem that their value is not being emphasized adequately. In this regard, an analysis of sample health-education documents provided by the agencies not only revealed great variation in their amount, range, and quality but also a lack of uniformity in the manner in which they are used for the training of foster parents. Thus, some of the study facilities reported that they have informal group discussions focusing on preventive health, others rely on nurse-foster-parent consultations, and a few utilize physician-foster-parent or caseworker-foster-parent meetings.

In general, the data obtained by the study team revealed that the health education of foster parents and the degree to which they are enlisted actively in the health supervision and treatment plan of their foster child is less than optimal. For example, providing foster parents with a foster child's placement history as well as behavioral and medical profile certainly would increase the possibility of a successful placement and enable the foster family to anticipate better the needs of the children in their care. However, more than half of the mothers interviewed remarked that they had not, at placement, been provided with information concerning the past history of the child. Moreover, in several instances, a child accepted into a particular home, on the basis of available information, was presumed to be well. Only later was it discovered that medical and/or emotional problems existed requiring frequent and often inconvenient visits over a lengthy course of treatment. In addition, almost half (45 percent) of the mothers reported that they never go to the agency clinic, 12 percent said they were never instructed how to meet their foster child's acute-illness needs, and only 54 percent said that the agency told them how to meet the child's needs for dental care. Also, one out of five mothers indicated that they (not the agency) decide when the child goes for dental care. However, when asked about their foster child's utilization of dental services, 19 percent said that their foster child never goes to the dentist.

The need for greater involvement of the foster family in the therapeutic program as well as the need for more-systematic and effective parent training is essential for the delivery of better levels of care. In fact, recent data indicate that attempts to provide parenting sessions that offer support, counseling, and guidance have given otherwise ill-prepared mothers and fathers a knowledge of basic parenting as well as an understanding of the special adjustment problems of children who a subjected to the trauma of separation.[31] It would seem that such groups should be compulsory, should meet routinely, and should include all individuals involved in the care of a particular child (that is, medical staff, parents, and caseworkers).

Moreover, useful intervention requires the development and dissemination of clearly and simply written information that describes all aspects of the medical, developmental, and dental needs of children and that highlights various preventive-care considerations. Such materials could detail the procedures for obtaining medical care, the schedule of routine medical and dental examinations, the program for immunizations, telephone numbers to call when necessary, potential alert signs of common childhood diseases, early-childhood and adolescent health problems, sociomedical concerns related to puberty and adolescence, accident prevention, nutrition, and proper utilization of pharmaceuticals and instruments like a thermometer.

Availability and Accessibility of Care. Among the mothers offering suggestions for change, the most frequent recommendation was for more geographically accessible service. Thus, 45 percent of this group maintained that the agency should let the foster mothers use local doctors and/or clinics, reflecting discontent with the requirement that certain of the child's needs be met directly at the headquarters clinic. The location of this facility was reported to be inconvenient by these mothers both in terms of traveling time, and availability of transportation. In addition, a number of respondents noted that the clinic hours were sometimes unsuitable, particularly if scheduled during the morning, because the mothers may have a great distance to travel or may have other children whom she must first dress, feed, and prepare for school. In fact, in our sample group, one-third reported that they had preschool children at home. Almost two-thirds (63 percent) said that they take these children along when the foster child goes for medical care, whereas 36 percent reported that they arrange for a babysitter. Although the inflexibility introduced by responsibility for several small children can be offset by access to babysitters in a child-care area at a health clinic or through other forms of reciprocity, such services are not widespread. This is unfortunate since some studies report the problem of child care as a barrier to the utilization of health services.[32] In our preliminary survey, referred to earlier, the difficulties with obtaining child care were found to be the most common reason for not visiting a doctor when there was illness among the study families.

In light of the difficulties inherent in the utilization of inconveniently located resources, it is conceivable that the lack of proximity of some services and the resultant difficulties could be a major situational deterrent to obtaining care. Thus, mothers who must travel long distances may not come in for care as early in illness or keep appointments as regularly as those who live closer to services. In this regard, it should be recognized that although Medicaid has eliminated the financial obstacles to obtaining care, it has not as yet focused on issues such as accessibility and availability. Thus, a recent survey of Medicaid programs revealed that several states offer health care through the schools and in day-care centers.[33] In New York State, in fact, the Board of Regents of New York State has proposed that routine physicals and immunizations be performed in the schools. Moreover, several pilot projects for in-school health care in New York City have been suggested.[34] Elsewhere, the Robert Wood Foundation has funded a number of innovative school health programs that provide more than just the basic preventive care.[35] These efforts indicate that it is possible to change the manner in which we deliver services to children so that they are more convenient and available.

In view of these comments as well as the previously documented high levels of need among these children, it certainly would seem that changes in the organization and structure of health services that would permit more-efficient utilization of resources also would encourage more-regular contact with physicans. Thus, if travel and waiting times could be minimized, then the mother's role as an escort would be less burdensome. This is particularly important for this population inasmuch as the medical-care responsibilities of these women, as noted earlier, often extend to a number of children, natural as well as foster. When we asked these mothers a number of questions regarding the utilization of ambulatory services among their own children as compared with their foster children, a number of interesting findings emerged. First, only 17 percent of the group reported that both their foster child and natural child had the same provider for routine and acute medical care, whereas another 19 percent indicated that the same provider was seen for only acute illnesses. However, two out of three respondents said the regular source of care for their own children was different than that for their foster children. For 54 percent, the provider was a private physician, and for 7 percent it was an outpatient department of a hospital. When asked which provider they preferred, 27 percent indicated the doctor the natural child saw, 13 percent replied the foster child's provider, and 45 percent had no preference. Some of the reasons given for their preference included comments such as "I know/trust/like/have confidence in the doctor"; "the office is conveniently located"; "I can communicate with the doctor"; and "there are short waits in the office."

In terms of dental care, four out of five respondents said that their natural child saw a private dentist, 16 percent indicated that a clinic was the source for dental care, and 3 percent replied no one usual place. Only one out of three of the mothers said that the same dental provider was used by both the natural and foster children. When asked which source of care they favored, 41 percent expressed a preference for the natural child's dentist, 6 percent preferred the foster child's dentist, and 52 percent had no preference.

Personal-Centered Care. A number of mothers also reported that a rushed atmosphere characterized some agency clinics, possibly indicative of examining physicians' highly limited time allotments to certain agencies. Then, too, it was mentioned that social workers, in some instances, were given responsibility for tasks that might best be provided by nursing personnel. A number of mothers also remarked that the doctors and nurses should take more of a personal interest in the children they serve. Also, several respondents said that attending physicians appeared condescending and somewhat paternalistic during clinic sessions, whereas other mothers observed that physicians and agency staff were not always willing to take the time to explain to the mother the proposed plan of treatment for her foster child.

In a related vein, foster mothers of children requiring services from hospital outpatient departments cited frequent and universally recognized dissatisfaction with long outpatient waiting-room time, staff inefficiency like misplaced charts, poor clinic atmosphere, inconvenience of clinic locations, and the occasionally questionable or abrupt attitudes of clinic staff toward foster parents and their children.

Completeness of Care. One out of three respondents expressed the view that the agency health program should be more thorough and that the agency should keep better track of the child's needs. Also, improved follow-up care was cited as a hoped-for change. In addition, 27 percent of the respondents agreed with the statement: The agency should meet the child's needs for mental-health care better than it does.

Foster-Mother Utilization of Services

The New York State Department of Social Services requires that all foster parents receive an initial physical examination and X-ray testing upon acceptance and that periodic X-ray screening (every three years) and annual medical re-examinations be obtained thereafter. Examination of responses obtained from the foster-mother interviews suggests, however, that the agencies neither ensure uniformly that state requirements for health examinations are fulfilled nor seem to inform foster mothers routinely that such requirements exist. Thus, when the study respondents were asked about agency regulations for routine health care, 12 percent said that as far as they knew, there were no such requirements, 8 percent replied that preventive examinations were to be obtained every two years, 1 percent said every three years, and 10 percent indicated that such testing was only performed at the time of the initial foster-family evaluation. Only 54 percent of the interviewees reported that the agency required that they have annual checkups in accordance with state regulations.

When the foster mothers were asked about their last visit to a doctor for a routine examination, only 62 percent said they had had such a visit during the preceding year, and another 27 percent said they never go for checkups. In a similar vein, a number of questions about screening for tuberculosis revealed that 11 percent of the respondents had not had a chest X-ray or tuberculosis test in over three years. Moreover, 6 percent of the group said that as far as they knew, there was no requirement for such testing, and 12 percent indicated that tuberculosis testing was only required at the time of foster-family acceptance.

In terms of dental care, 55 percent of the mothers said that they had visited a dentist in the preceding year, 12 percent replied over one year ago, but 28 percent said they never go for routine dental examinations and only utilize dental services when there is pain and/or obvious oral pathology requiring treatment.

When asked about illness-related visits, approximately two out of three respondents said that they always see a doctor when sick, and another 27 percent said that they avoid visiting the doctor when ill for a variety of reasons including "costs too much," "it's inconvenient," "too much trouble," and "don't like doctors." In a related vein, the mothers were asked to describe the health-care arrangements they would prefer to have for their family, if they had a choice. In response to this item, the most favored arrangement was reported to be one private doctor to treat the whole family (44 percent). This was followed by a preference for several private doctors, including one for adults and one for children (31 percent), and last, by a clinic of a large hospital that has the equipment necessary for all kinds of examinations (19 percent).

In terms of health-insurance coverage, about two-thirds (64 percent) of the respondents indicated that they had some form of insurance through either their place of work or private coverage, and most of the group responding to this item said that it was adequate to meet their family's needs. However, 8 percent reported that they had no health insurance, and another 28 percent did not respond to this item.

Summary

The analysis in this chapter was based on the replies of a sample of New York City foster mothers to a survey of their attitudes and perceptions concerning the health status and needs of their foster children and the adequacy of services provided to this population. The interviewees, in many respects, resemble other low-income New York City residents, but their association with the foster-care agencies and the responsibilities incurred because of this association may have influenced their attitudes and practices with regard to health behavior. Accordingly, care must be taken in any comparisons with other populations. Mindful of these limitations, our principal findings follow.

The majority of mothers exhibited an essentially positive view of their foster child's health status. Compared with respondents from other populations, they were more likely to assess his or her health in favorable terms and were less likely to acknowledge poor health. Contrasted with mothers from other survey groups, they were more likely to be concerned or worried about their foster child's health. Behavioral/emotional problems were cited as the principal cause of their concern, yet only a minority indicated that appropriate care had been obtained.

Utilization of medical services (as measured by total number of doctor-patient contacts for a twelve-month period) was reported by these mothers to be slightly lower than the levels reported for national samples. Since the children in this study were found upon examination to be less healthy than comparably aged children from more widely based study groups, one might expect them to exhibit higher levels of utilization than these other children. Data gathered during the physical-examination and record-review phases of this study revealed, however, a low level of utilization for these foster children as well as large numbers of medically unattended problems.

Usual health-care patterns identified for these children by their foster mothers suggest continuity of care through a consistently high reliance on agency clinics and agency-assigned doctors for preventive service. Thus, three out of four interviewees maintained that their foster child regularly sees the same agency-affiliated doctor for checkups. However, FCHS record data indicated that the source of care for routine examinations was not constant—only 9 percent of the sampled children apparently had seen the same doctor for checkups during the five years preceding the study—and that care was not monitored carefully; that is, preschoolers were found to have inadequate levels of immunization, simple laboratory and sensory screening tests were not routinely performed and recorded, and referral and follow-up care was frequently haphazard. A high estimate of dental health and dental utilization was reported by respondents for their study children; nearly all the interviewees maintained that their foster-care charges received dental checkups regularly; only one in five acknowledged that their foster child never goes. However, an examination of related FCHS data drawn from the medical records and dental-screening tests shows that close to half the study children were classified by dental evaluators as in need of treatment. Furthermore, nearly half of those referred for care had not been to a dentist in the last five years. These findings suggest, despite the reports of these respondents, that dental care has not been promptly, consistently, or adequately provided.

Responses to general evaluative questions about agency medical programs with respect to the quality of care, its comprehensiveness, and the personal manner in which it was given revealed high overall satisfaction with the services provided. However, several specific inquiries disclosed concern in such areas as agencies' failure to provide birth or health-history data prior to a child's placement; advice concerning aspects such as first aid, home safety, proper nutrition, or the treatment of common illnesses; guidelines describing health-care procedures for preventive and general health management; more geographically accessible and available resources; more-thorough care; better follow-up; and more-personalized services.

Although the overall pattern of responses presented here can be construed as essentially positive, the specific variables studied and the themes emerged suggest several deficiencies in knowledge and care that should not be overlooked. Thus, as noted, the health examinations and record reviews performed for this study revealed that many of these children are in need of high levels of comprehensive and specialized care. However, their inability to make consistent use of available resources in appropriate ways suggests that some of their surrogate parents have not been informed sufficiently about preventive and therapeutic measures and that they have not attended consistently to general health management to the extent that would seem desirable. If adequate care is to become a reality, then more-effective educational techniques that would enable agencies to guide foster parents regarding the health needs of their charges should be instituted. Perhaps the routine utilization of individual and group health-orientation sessions, using appropriate and thoughtfully designed health literature (simple, colloquially written and illustrated, offering immunization, dietary advice, and well-child counseling, and so forth), is worthy of exploration. Further, agencies should encourage continuing communication and provide ongoing assistance, support, and follow-up services to these mothers. These steps, together with systematic and persistent monitoring activities should serve to engender a program of care that is adaptable and responsive to the needs of these children.

Notes

1. Francis C. Lindaman, "Staff Training and the Working Relationships of Providers and Consumers in Spanish Harlem," *American Journal of Public Health* 60 (July 1970):1225–1229.

2. G.M. Hochbaum, "Consumer Participation in Health Planning," *American Journal of Public Health* 59 (September 1969):1698–1705.

3. N.K. Gray et al., "Advocates for Change in T.B. Treatment and Control," *American Journal of Public Health* 61 (December 1971): 2384–2386.

4. David Mechanic, "The Influence of Mothers on Their Children's Health, Attitudes and Behavior," *Pediatrics* 33 (March 1964):444–453.

5. See, for example, Eugenia S. Carpenter, "Children's Health Care and the Changing Role of Women," *Medical Care* 18 (December 1980): 1208–1218; and L. Pratt, "Child Rearing Methods and Children's Health Behavior," *Journal of Health and Social Behavior* 14 (1973):61.

6. L. Aday and R. Eichorn, *The Utilization of Health Services and Correlates. A Research Bibliography,* DHEW pub. no. (HSM) 73–300 3 (Rockville, Md.: National Center for Health Services Research and Development, 1973); A. Booth and N. Babchuk, "Seeking Health Care from New Resources," *Journal of Health and Social Behavior* 13 (1972):90; and T.J. Litman, "Health Care and the Family: A Three Generational Analysis," *Medical Care* 9 (1971):67.

7. Edward A. Suchman, "Health Orientations and Medical Care," *American Journal of Public Health* 56 (January 1966):97–105.

8. D. Rosenblatt and Edward A. Suchman, "Blue-Collar Attitudes and Information toward Health and Illness," in *Blue Collar World,* eds. Arthur Shostak and William Gomberg (Englewood Cliffs, N.J.: Prentice-Hall, 1964), pp. 324–333; Earl Loman Koos, *The Health of Regionville* (New York: Columbia University Press, 1954); H.E. Freeman and C. Lambert, Jr., "Preventive Behavior of Urban Mothers," *Journal of Health and Human Behavior* 6 (1965):141; and Serena E. Wade, "Trends in Public Knowledge about Health and Illness," *American Journal of Public Health* 60 (March 1970):485–491.

9. David Fanshel, *Foster Parenthood: A Role Analysis* (Minneapolis: University of Minnesota Press, 1966); Henry S. Maas, ed., *Research in the Social Services: A Five-Year Review* (New York: National Association of Social Workers, 1971), pp. 46–49; and D. Taylor and P. Starr, "Foster Parenting: An Integrative Review of the Literature," *Child Welfare,* 46 (1967).

10. National Center for Health Statistics, *Medical Care, Health Status, and Family Income,* Public Health Service pub. no. 1000 (Washington, D.C.: Government Printing Office, 1965).

11. Lois Pratt, "The Relationship of Socioeconomic Status to Health," *American Journal of Public Health* 61 (February 1971):281–291; and Jeanette Rayner, "Socioeconomic Status and Factors Influencing the Dental Health Practices of Mothers," *American Journal of Public Health* 60 (July 1970):1250–1258.

12. Koos, *The Health of Regionville.*

13. Lola M. Irelan, ed., *Low-Income Life Styles* (Washington, D.C.:

DHEW, Social and Rehabilitation Service, Office of Research and Demonstration, 1971).

14. Freeman and Lambert, "Preventive Behavior"; Eugene B. Gallagher, "Prenatal and Infant Care in a Medium-Sized Community," *American Journal of Public Health* 57 (1967):2127–2137; R.B. Nolan, J.L. Schwartz, and K. Simonian, "Social Class Differences in Utilization of Pediatric Services in a Prepaid Direct Service Medical Program,"*American Journal of Public Health* 57 (January 1967):34–47; and L.C. Deasy, "Socio-Economic Status and Participation in the Poliomyelitis Vaccine Trial," *American Sociological Review* (April 1956), pp. 185–191.

15. Edward A. Suchman, "Social Patterns of Illness and Medical Care," *Journal of Health and Human Behavior* 6 (Spring 1965):2–16; and Suchman, "Socio-Medical Variations among Ethnic Groups," *American Journal of Sociology* 60 (November 1964):319–331.

16. H.P. Anderson, *The Bracero Program in California,* mimeographed (Los Angeles: University of California School of Public Health, 1961); and M.A. Glasser, "A Study of the Public's Acceptance of the Salk Vaccine Program," *American Journal of Public Health* 48 (1958):141–146.

17. Lawrence Podell, "Utilization of Health Services by Welfare Recipients: Basic Cross-Tabulators" (Unpublished report to the National Center for Health Services Research and Development, Washington, D.C., 1969); and National Center for Health Statistics, *Examination and Health History Findings among Children and Youths, 6–17 Years.* Series 11, no. 129, DHEW pub. no. (HRA) 74–1611 Health Resources Administration (Washington, D.C.: Government Printing Office, November 1973).

18. National Center for Health Statistics, *Examination and Health History.*

19. National Center for Health Statistics, *Physicians Volume and Interval Since Last Visit. United States—1975,* (Vital and Health Statistics Series 10, no. 128, DHEW pub. no. (PHS) 79–1556 (Rockville, Md., 1979).

20. National Center for Health Statistics, *Current Estimates from the Health Interview Survey—United States 1972,* Vital and Health Statistics Series 10, no. 85, DHEW pub. no. (HRA) 74–1512, Health Resources Administration (Washington, D.C., September 1973).

21. Steven L. Gortmaker, "Medicaid and the Health Care of Children in Poverty and Near Poverty," *Medical Care* 19 (June 1981):567–582; R.W. Wilson and E.L. White, "Changes in Morbidity, Disability, and Utilization Differentials between the Poor and Nonpoor: Data from the Health Interview Survey 1964–1973," *Medical Care* 15 (1977):636; and Suezanne Tangerose Orr, and C. Arden Miller, "Utilization of Health Services by Poor Children since Advent of Medicaid," *Medical Care* 19 (June 1981): 583–590.

22. Gortmaker, "Medicaid and the Health Care of Children."

23. Wilson and White, "Changes in Morbidity"; and Orr and Miller, "Utilization of Health Services."

24. J. Kronenfield, "The Medicaid Program and a Regular Source of Care," *American Journal of Public Health* 68 (1978):771.

25. National Center for Health Statistics and National Center for Health Services Research, *Health, United States, 1976–77,* DHEW pub. no. (HRA) 77–1232 Hyattsville, Md., 1977.

26. Gortmaker, "Medicaid and the Health Care of Children."

27. American Academy of Pediatrics, *Lengthening Shadows* (Report of the Council on Pediatric Practice of the American Academy of Pediatrics on the Delivery of Health Care to Children, Evanston, Ill.: 1971).

28. Chicago Indigent Dental Survey, 1960. Reported in Chicago Board of Health, *Preliminary Report on Patterns of Medical and Health Care in Poverty Areas of Chicago and Proposed Health Programs for the Medically Indigent* (Chicago, 1965).

29. A.F. North, "Project Head Start and the Pediatrician," *Clinical Pediatrics* 6 (April 1967):191–194.

30. National Center for Health Statistics: *Decayed, Missing and Filled Teeth among Children—United States,* Vital and Health Statistics Series 11, no. 106, Health Service and Mental Health Administration (Washington, D.C.: Government Printing Office, August 1971); and National Center for Health Statistics, *Decayed, Missing and Filled Teeth among Youths 12–17 Years—United States,* Vital and Health Statistics Series 11, no. 144, Health Resources Administration (Washington, D.C.: Government Printing Office, October 1974).

31. Suand B. Campbell et al., "Successful Foster Homes Need Parent-Child Match," *Journal of Social Welfare,* 6, no. 2 (Fall/Winter 1979–1980):49.

32. S.S. Bellin and H.J. Geiger, "The Impact of a Neighborhood Health Center on Patient Behavior and Attitudes Relating to a Housing Project," *Medical Care* 10 (May–June 1972):224–239; and Lawrence Podell and Richard Pomeroy, *Studies in the Use of Health Services by Families on Welfare* (New York: Center of the Study of Urban Problems, City University of New York, April 1970).

33. H.M. Wallace, H. Goldstein, and A.C. Oglesby, "The Health and Medical Care of Children under Title 19 (Medicaid)," *American Journal of Public Health* 64 (1974):568.

34. A. Goldman, "Regents Propose Establishing Clinics for In-School Health Care of Students," *The New York Times,* November 15, 1979, p. B1 (col. 5).

35. Robert Wood Johnson Foundation, *School Health Services,* Special Report no. 11 (Princeton, N.J., 1979).

8 Factors Affecting Health-Care Costs

The magnitude of health-care expenditures in the United States for the over 500,000 children receiving foster-care services is vast and rising sharply and steadily. During the year in which this study was conducted, 1973–1974, the outlay of public funds by federal, state, and local governments for health services for these children exceeded $200 million.[1] In New York City alone, costs exceeded $22 million for some 28,000 children in placement during the study year,[2] and figures for 1981 show that public funds expended in this area (excluding inpatient and outpatient services) totaled $30 million (table 8-1).[3]

A major purpose of our study was to examine the relationships between the cost of care, the health needs of the children, and the structure and functioning of existing medical-care programs provided by the New York City agencies that assume responsibility for the children. This chapter addresses the issue of health-care costs. The objective is to determine the basis for the differences in the costs of providing medical care by examining those factors that demonstrate a statistical association with agency per capita costs. As a starting point for this analysis, a theoretical framework was established. As outlined, this framework suggests factors that could account for the observed variations in annual per capita costs among the study facilities (see chapter 2).[4]

Thus, interagency cost differentials might be affected by interagency differences in the structure and organization of the care system, the quality and adequacy of care provided, and the health statuses and medical-care needs of the children. We must acknowledge that a large and unknown proportion of interagency variability might also be attributed to the so-called noise factor of errors in measurement and scaling and to variables not identified. In addition, each of the preceding suggested dimensions offers its own problems in delineation and measurement. For example, the quality of care a child receives is difficult to define, either conceptually or operationally, as is the health status of a population. It may be assumed, then, that

---

The results of the cost analysis presented here have been published in Margaret R. Swire and Florence Kavaler, "Health Services for Foster Children: Factors Associated with Health Care Costs," *Journal of Health, Politics and Law* 3 (Summer 1978):251–263.

Table 8-1
Medical Expenditures for Children in Foster Care in New York City,
1970-1980

Year	Number of New York City Public Charges in Foster Care[a]	Dollar Amount of Expenditures[b]
1970-1971	26,514	10,277,472
1971-1972	27,704	11,902,545
1972-1973	28,068	14,111,577
1973-1974	28,690	16,647,436
1980-1981	23,664	30,000,000

Note: Figures exclude inpatient and outpatient hospital care.

[a] New York City Department of Social Services, "Summary Analysis of Monthly Population Reports Submitted by Foster Care Agencies; Children Remaining in Care, 1970-1974," mimeographed (New York).

[b] New York State Department of Social Services, Division of Medical Assistance (Albany, N.Y., 1981). These figures include the cost of medical care for children in foster boarding homes, institutions, group homes, and residences. Figures for 1970-1974 derive from schedules D and E, State Claims Division, New York State Department of Social Services. Figures for 1980-1981 are based on data provided by the Division of Medical Assistance, New York State Department of Social Services.

some amount of variability in the results will be due to methodological problems, and readers should bear these limitations in mind.

Data Analysis

Grouping of Variables

A set of sixty-six variables was chosen for this analysis and was classified as follows:

Background Variables. This group of seven variables describes the socio-demographic characteristics of the subjects as well as their placement histories, including age, sex, race, and religion of these children, age at placement, reason for placement, and length of stay in care.

1. Sex of study child
2. Race of study child
3. Age of child on day of clinical examination

4. Religion of study child
5. Reason for placement
6. Year of admission to agency
7. Number of years in care with agency

Medical-Care Structure Variables. This group of twenty-eight variables involves organizational, administrative, and financial aspects of agency care programs. Derived from data gathered during the record survey as well as from agency statistical, cost, and population reports, these items provide measures of the cost of care (for example, total Medicaid per capita costs; the proportion of these costs that reflects in-house medical, mental-, and dental-health services); the numbers of in-house medical, mental-health, and ancillary staff; how they organized (for example, centralized versus decentralized); and patterns of services (for example, preventive, acute-, and specialty-care utilization rates by site of service).

8. Annual acute-illness-visit rate
9. Annual acute-illness-visit rate to in-house providers
10. Annual acute-illness-visit rate to community practitioners
11. Annual actue-illness-visit rate: Ratio of in-house to total visits
12. Annual preventive-care-visit rate to in-house providers
13. Annual preventive-care-visit rate to community practitioners
14. Annual preventive-care-visit rate: Ratio of in-house to total visits
15. Annual specialty-care-visit rate to in-house providers
16. Annual specialty-care-visit rate to community practitioners
17. Annual specialty-care-visit rate: Ratio of in-house to total visists
18. Annual rate of referral visits per study child (excludes dental)
19. Annual visit rate to psychiatrists and psychologists
20. Hospitalization episodes for period 1968–1973
21. Number of days hospitalized for period 1968–1973
22. Agency
23. Medicaid per capita costs
24. Medical per capita costs (excludes dental and mental-health costs)
25. Multifunctional structure (Number and percent of case load in institutional group home or other type placement)
26. Case-load age distribution (percent under six years)
27. Medicaid costs: percent indirect
28. Medicaid costs: percent in-house (versus community)
29. Mental-health costs: percent in-house (versus community)
30. Dental costs: percent in-house (versus community)
31. In-house medical-clinic hours per week
32. Medical-director hours per week
33. Number of in-house medical and ancillary staff

34. Number of in-house staff psychiatrists and psychologists
35. Number of in-house hours budgeted for psychiatric and psychological care

Medical-Care Process Variables. This group consists of twenty-two performance variables that are used as measures of the quality or adequacy of care provided to agency clientele. Of these, fourteen record the extent and thoroughness of preventive services as well as the effectiveness of referral and follow-up procedures. These derive from medical-record data. The remaining eight variables in this group are qualitative in that they reflect features of care such as the degree of agency supervision over the child's care program, the extent to which control of medical records resides in the hands of medical staff or social-work personnel, the organization of medical records (scaled from good to poor), the extent to which record information was current (from current to not current), and the quality of referral feedback (excellent to poor). Ratings assigned to agencies for each of these items were based on the pooled judgments of project reviewers, their supervisor, and the project administrator. Although in large measure these ratings reflect the experiences of the record reviewers, they also derive from information obtained during site visit appraisals and interviews conducted with administrative and medical personnel.

36. Admission examination: Ninety records with no recorded evidence
37. Annual preventive-care-visit rate
38. Admission-examination-component rate
39. Examination preventive-component rate
40. Immunization level: actual number recorded in record, 1968–1973
41. Annual tuberculin-screening-test rate
42. Annual hemoglobin/hematocrit-screening-test rate
43. Annual urinalysis-screening-test rate
44. Annual dental-screening-test rate
45. Annual vision-screening-test rate
46. Annual hearing-screening-test rate
47. Referral-recommended rate
48. Referral-accomplished rate
49. Ratio of referrals accomplished to referrals recommended
50. Degree of agency supervision over child's medical-care program
51. Agency medical-department (versus foster-mother) control over child's utilization of services
52. Medical-department (versus social worker) control of medical records
53. Organization of medical records
54. Time required to perform audit
55. Degree to which record information is current

56. Immunization record system
57. Quality of referral feedback

Medical-Care Outcome Variables. This group of nine variables is comprised of various measures of the physical, mental, and dental health of the study subjects. Based on the findings of the clinical-examination survey, these items reflect the following: physician's clinical impressions of health status, referrals recommended for specialty treatment, visual-acuity levels, hearing impairment levels, dental-treatment needs, developmental and mental-health statuses, and verbal intelligence levels.

58. Physician global impression of health
59. Physician referrals recommended for specialty treatment
60. Visual acuity without correction
61. Visual acuity with correction
62. Hearing-test results
63. Dental-treatment needs
64. Peabody Picture Vocabulary Test results
65. Denver Developmental Test rating
66. Psychiatric-impairment rating

Multiple Correlation Matrix

These sixty-six items were correlated and an interrelation matrix was developed. Analysis of the association between these measures was then carried out using a cluster-analysis procedure since this method yielded the best understanding of the relationships between these variables.[a]

---

[a] Cluster analysis is a technique that yields clusters of variables that are more like one another than they are like variables in other clusters. The linkage is determined by the largest index of association that a single variable has with any or all other variables, or more generally, it is the highest correlation a variable has with a composite of all the characteristics of the members of a cluster.

Thus, the core of the first cluster will be the two variables in the entire matrix that are linked by the highest correlation coefficient. These two variables each attach to themselves other variables in that their linkage is the highest index of association exhibited by these secondary measures. Third and fourth levels of clustering can occur if each of these newly linked variables in turn attracts still other variables by their corresponding highest order correlation coefficients. Finally, clusters arise in which the members resemble one another more closely than they do members of other clusters. In the following analysis a highly meaningful picture emerges, a result which does not always occur with factor analysis. For a more-detailed discussion of this procedure, see Louis L. McQuitty, "Elementary Linkage Analysis for Isolating Orthogonal and Oblique Types and Typal Relevancies," *Educational and Psychological Measurement* 17 (1957):207–229; and R. Tyron and D. Bailey, *Cluster Analysis* (New York: McGraw-Hill, 1970).

Clusters I, II, and III, the most powerful clusters to emerge from the analysis, are presented and interpreted in the following sections.

Cluster I. In Cluster I, the strongest cluster to arise from this analysis, we have a grouping of variables designating the administrative character of the agencies (see figure 8-1). The agencies $(A_1)^b$ are sharply distinguished from one another by the completeness of their medical records (as measured by A_2—the time required to audit those records)^c and also by administrative features such as the degree to which they supervise the child's medical-care program (B_{22}), the type of staff (medical versus social work) that controls their record systems (B_{12}), the extent to which their health expenditures reflect indirect rather than direct care services (B_{23}), the degree to which their health costs are accounted for by in-house rather than community-care services (B_{11}), and the extent to which their medical records show evidence of admission examination information (B_{21}). Though less prominent, other items implicated in this cluster measure the degree to which the agencies maintain an in-house staff of medical professionals (C_{121}, D_{124}), the extent to which they provide centralized clinic services (D_{123}), the degree to which their mental- and dental-health costs reflect in-house expenditures (C_{122}, D_{121}), the frequency with which they refer their clientele for specialty care $(C_{11(1)}, C_{11(2)})$, and the religious distribution of their case loads (D_{122}). That the latter is involved in this predominantly administrative cluster implies that agencies that function under specific religious auspices (and six do: three are Catholic, two are Protestant, and one is Jewish) tend to have distinct administrative structures. That this correlation should be relatively weak (0.23) is also noteworthy in that the clientele served are not always of the same religious persuasion as the agency.

In short, then, this grouping of variables suggests that agencies that tend to have complete health records also tend to have medical rather than social-work personnel in charge of these records. Further, they are more likely to maintain close supervision over the child's care, are more likely to provide services on an in-house basis, and are more likely to have higher per capita in-house expenditures than those agencies that have looser control of care, less-complete records, and a higher reliance on outside services for the provision of care.

---

^{b} The symbolism used consistently throughout this exposition is as follows. The two core variables of each cluster are labeled A_1 and A_2. Whatever variables are linked on the next level are labeled B, with subscripts designating linkage to the corresponding core variables. Thus, if two second variables are linked to A_2, these are designated B_{21} and B_{22}. Third-level variables are lettered C, and fourth-level variables are D, with appropriate subscripts indicating their linkages.

^{c} The more time required to audit the record, the more inclusive the chart.

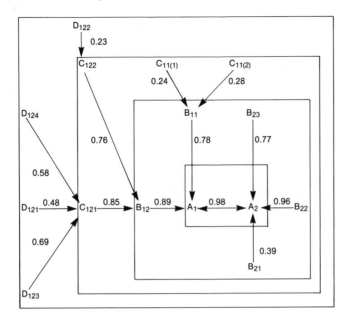

Variables

A_1	=	Agency
A_2	=	Time required to perform audit
B_{11}	=	Medicaid costs: Percent in-house (versus community)
B_{12}	=	Medical-department (versus social-worker) control of medical records
B_{21}	=	Admission examination: no recorded evidence
B_{22}	=	Agency supervision over child's medical-care program
B_{23}	=	Medicaid costs: Percent indirect
$C_{11(1)}$	=	Referral-recommended rate
$C_{11(2)}$	=	Referral-accomplished rate
C_{121}	=	Percent in-house medical and ancillary staff
C_{122}	=	Mental-health costs: Percent in-house (versus community)
D_{121}	=	Dental costs: Percent in-house (versus community)
D_{122}	=	Religion of study child
D_{123}	=	In-house medical-clinic hours per week
D_{124}	=	Medical-director hours per week

Source: Florence Kavaler and Margaret R. Swire, ''Health Services for Foster Children: Factors Associated with Health Care Costs,'' *Journal of Health Politics, Policy, and Law.* 3, no. 2 (Summer 1978):251–263. Reprinted with permission.

Figure 8–1. Cluster I Variables

Cluster II. Turning to Cluster II (figure 8–2), we find that the dominant content, as with Cluster I, is conveyed by structural aspects of the care system. The major factors associated with health care costs (A_1) measure the extent to which the agency provides in-house mental-health services

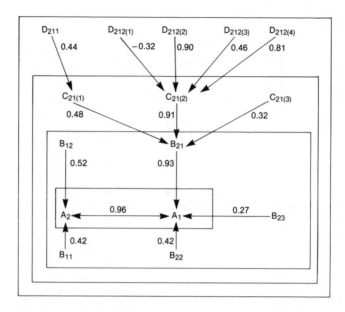

Source: Florence Kavaler and Margaret R. Swire, "Health Services for Foster Children: Factors Associated with Health Care Costs," *Journal of Health Politics, Policy, and Law* 3, no. 2 (Summer 1978):251–263. Reprinted with permission.

Figure 8–2. Cluster II Variables

Variables

A_1	=	Medicaid per capita costs (includes medical, dental, and mental-health costs)
A_2	=	Percent in-house budgeted for psychiatric and psychological service
B_{11}	=	Annual tuberculin-screening-test rate
B_{12}	=	Annual preventive-care-visit rate: Ratio of in-house to total visits
B_{21}	=	Multifunctional structure
B_{22}	=	Annual vision-screening-test rate
B_{23}	=	Annual acute-illness-visit rate: Ratio of in-house to total visits
$C_{21(1)}$	=	Annual urinalysis-screening-test rate
$C_{21(2)}$	=	Percent in-house staff psychiatrists and psychologists
$C_{21(3)}$	=	Ratio of referrals accomplished to referrals recommended
D_{211}	=	Annual hemoglobin/hematocrit-screening-test rate
$D_{212(1)}$	=	Race of study child
$D_{212(2)}$	=	Degree to which record information is current
$D_{212(3)}$	=	Annual dental-screening-test rate
$D_{212(4)}$	=	Immunization record system

(A₂), the degree to which the agency is multi- or unifunctional (B_{21}) in structure, and the extent to which the agency provides in-house preventive health care (B_{12}). [A multifunctional organization offers an array of services (for example, group home, boarding home, residential treatment center, and institution) whereas a unifunctional facility offers only a single type of service.] Vision (B_{22}), tuberculin (B_{11}), and urinalysis ($C_{21(1)}$) screening-test levels are also involved in the cost picture as are such variables as the frequency of in-house acute-care visits (B_{23}), the number of in-house mental-health professionals ($C_{21(2)}$), and the ratio of referrals accomplished to those recommended ($C_{21(3)}$). Other less-prominent items in this cluster reflect the degree to which recorded medical information is current ($D_{212(2)}$), the adequacy of the immunization record-keeping system ($D_{212(4)}$), the frequency with which dental screening is performed ($D_{212(3)}$), and the ethnic distribution of the case load ($D_{212(1)}$). These relationships suggest that agencies that have large numbers of in-house mental-health professionals also tend to have more-complete and up-to-date immunization data and general health information in their records, as well as higher levels of dental screening and larger numbers of white and Puerto Rican children under care.

In sum, a picture emerges that clarifies the relationship between the cost of care on the one hand and various components of care on the other. Agencies that have high per capita health costs tend to be multifunctional and centralized in terms of their health-care organization. These same agencies tend to have more-thorough levels of testing and screening, more-effective systems for record-keeping, and higher rates of medical follow-through than facilities that have low per capita costs.

Cluster III. In Cluster III, we have a group of variables that further delineates the relationship between the cost of medical care and various characteristics of the care program. As may be seen in figure 8–3, the factor most clearly associated with, and thus a good index of, medical-care costs (A_2) (excluding dental and mental-health costs) is the one that measures record-keeping effectiveness (A_1)—namely, the quality of referral feedback (that is, the extent to which reports retrieved from specialty-care providers are current and complete). Other items in this cluster linked with medical-care costs reflect the degree to which the agency medical department (rather than the foster mother) controls the child's utilization of services (B_{21}), the frequency of in-house specialty-care visits (B_{22}, $C_{22(1)}$), the extent to which medical-record data is well organized (B_{11}), the completeness of the admission examination and subsequent preventive health examinations (D_{21}, E_{21}), and the age distribution of the case load ($C_{21(1)}$).

Viewed overall, this cluster provides a picture that is in accord with earlier findings about structural aspects of the care program and their effects on cost. In brief, agencies with high medical costs tend to have better-organized medical records, more-adequate referral feedback systems, more control over the child's utilization of services, more-frequent use of in-house speciality-care services, a more-thorough approach to preventive health supervision, and a higher proportion of preschool clientele comprising their case loads than agencies with lower costs.

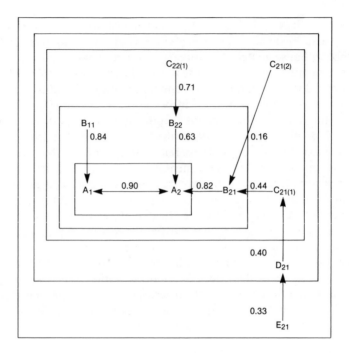

Variables

A_1 = Quality of referral feedback
A_2 = Medical per capita costs (excludes dental and mental-health costs)
B_{11} = Organization of medical records
B_{21} = Agency medical-department (versus foster-mother) control over child's utilization
          of services
B_{22} = Annual specialty-care-visit rate to in-house providers
$C_{21(1)}$ = Case-load age distribution: percent under six years of age
$C_{21(2)}$ = Reason for placement
$C_{22(1)}$ = Annual specialty-care-visit rate: Ratio of in-house to total visits
D_{21} = Preventive-examination-component rate
E_{21} = Admission-examination-component rate

Source: Florence Kavaler and Margaret R. Swire, "Health Services for Foster Children:
Factors Associated with Health Care Costs," *Journal of Health Politics, Policy, and Law* 3,
no. 2 (Summer 1978):251–263. Reprinted with permission.

Figure 8–3. Cluster III Variables

Summary

This chapter describes the results of a cluster-analysis procedure that was
used to examine the relationships among the costs of care, the health needs
of the children, and the structure and functioning of existing medical-care

programs. Since the findings are merely correlational, they do not, strictly speaking, establish a causal direction. Nonetheless, they do have explanatory power and provide results that have broad implications for the delivery of foster-care health services. Most important, our analyses showed that the major factors associated with health-care costs are structural and functional. We found that high per capita costs tend to be associated with agency features such as multifunctionalism; centralization of health-care services; large numbers of in-house medical and mental-health staff; accurate, thorough, and up-to-date records; close control over these records; close supervision of the child's medical-care program; better, more-frequent, and more-complete preventive health checkups; and higher frequency of screening and diagnostic testing. It was not possible, however, to demonstrate any relationship between the health status of the children and the per capita cost of providing medical care.

Notes

1. Department of Health, Education, and Welfare, *Medical Assistance, (Medicaid) financed under Title XIX of the Social Security Act* (Washington, D.C.: Government Printing Office, 1974).

2. New York State Department of Social Services, *Statistical Reports on Vendor Medical Care, 1974* (Albany, N.Y., 1974), schedules D and E State Claims Division. These figures include payments to physicians, dentists, podiatrists, and clinical laboratories.

3. New York State Department of Social Services, Division of Medical Assistance, *Gross Medicaid Reimbursement for Fiscal 1980–1981* (Albany, N.Y., 1982) (excludes inpatient and outpatient hospital costs).

4. Variations in 1973–1974 costs between the study agencies were quite large, ranging from a low of $83 per child per year to a high of $773 per child per year.

9 Conclusion

The system for providing health care to foster children is woefully inadequate, both in New York State and in the country. In a sense, the foster child has not one but four sets of inadequate parents: the natural mother and father, the state (and, in most cases, the city) agencies, the foster-care agencies, and the foster parents. This trilevel hierarchical system of surrogate parents is intended to ensure the health of the child, with the state overseeing the entire system, the foster-care agencies providing medical and psychiatric care, and the foster parents supervising and caring for the child on a day-to-day basis. This division of responsibilities is appropriate and could result in proper care if the following conditions did not exist: (1) the existing (and often inadequate) state guidelines are not adhered to or enforced; (2) the standards of the different foster agencies vary and, in addition, are often ignored by staff; and (3) the foster parents sometimes are selected poorly and often misperceive or ignore the health status of their foster children. In fact, when a child is taken from natural parents who are of lower socioeconomic status, poorly educated, physically or psychologically impaired, and/or abusive, he or she may be placed with foster parents who also possess many of these characteristics. The child often continues to be abused or neglected, and his physical or emotional problems continue to go untreated. The foster-care system as it exists is a tangle of misplaced, confused, and/or ignored responsibilities. Often no one in the system knows who is responsible for an aspect of the care of a child, with the result that no one takes responsibility and the child suffers.

By failing to deal with the medical and psychiatric problems of foster children, the system, as Fanshel suggests, may be ensuring its continued existence by producing the next generation of inadequate and impaired parents.[1]

To arrest this insidious cycle, changes must be made at all three levels of the system. In New York City, the site of this survey, the state of New York does not closely supervise the organizations, for the most part private agencies, to whom foster children are entrusted. The state does not insist that these agencies follow any single set of health-care guidelines. Not one of the fourteen agencies examined in this survey adhered to the New York State Department of Social Services guidelines, compliance with which supposedly is required. All of the agencies had written guidelines, yet these varied considerably from one organization to another. Perhaps one could argue that agency flexibility is the goal of the state, but if this were the case, one would expect the state at least to oversee the determination and revision of agency standards. The state does not do this. In some cases the formulation and revision of agency policies are the sole responsibility of the agency's medical director.

Given the state's abdication of role as the formulator and enforcer of policy, control essentially passes to the next lower level in the hierarchy, the agencies. Do the agencies accept systematic programs to ensure adequate care? The data suggest that they do not. When agency children were evaluated in this survey, the rate of medical problems and developmental and psychological impairments was markedly greater than among non-foster-care children. This higher level of health deficiency is in part a residual effect of the child's poor upbringing in the natural family, but not entirely. Even after children enter the foster-care system, health care continues to be disorganized and ineffective. For example, 47 percent of the children found is this survey to have a visual-acuity disorder had not seen an ophthalmologist in the preceding five years, much of that time in foster care. Three-quarters of the survey children with emotional or developmental problems had not seen a counselor during the same period. If one can assume that visual, emotional, and developmental difficulties have a detrimental effect on a child's maturation and schooling, then agency health care is indeed helping to provide the next generation of indigent adults.

A major source of difficulty at the agency level is the lack of centralized control within each agency. Although the New York State Department of Social Services requires that each agency have a medical director, preferably a pediatrician, two of the fourteen agencies had no director, and one had only a nominal director whose primary function was that of a chief psychiatrist. Of the other eleven, the majority had directors who served between three hours per month and six hours per week. As the data quoted here and throughout this book indicate, it is impossible to supervise adequately the care of hundreds of needy children in absentia. Standards for treatment are not necessarily made specific enough to replace a director's guidance. In addition, often neither the New York State Department of Social Services guidelines nor the in-house standards that exist are communicated (distributed) effectively to staff and foster parents.

One result of this absence of control is that medical records are lost or incomplete and, thus, that a child's health needs are either never discovered, forgotten, or ignored. In practice, the scheduling of initial and follow-up visits to doctors and the keeping of medical records often becomes the responsibility of the caseworker. However, caseworkers apparently tend to underemphasize the importance of a child's physical needs. Dental care serves as a good example. Ten of the agencies use outside practitioners in this field, with record keeping the responsibility of the caseworker or in-house secretary. This study found that follow-up care soon became haphazard. Foster children had four times the rate of dental caries as children in the general population.

Some of the problems with record keeping may be attributed to the local practitioners used by foster children. Many make a practice of turning in incomplete medical forms. If outside practitioners are to be used, the agency should be responsible for getting, and keeping track of, thorough records. Moreover, an agency should take steps to ensure that its children see worthy practitioners and should encourage foster parents to continue to take children to the same practitioner if a good one is found. Currently, the agencies do neither. In choosing a local practitioner, the agency often uses no other cirterion than the recommendation of the foster mother, and only 9 percent of the survey children saw the same doctor twice for a checkup during the five years preceding the survey. Such nomadic tendencies mandate that caseworkers be all the more assiduous in keeping track of the child's medical records. Although these examples show the extent of caseworker neglect of the physical needs of the foster children in their charge, one should not be misled; this study clearly shows that caseworkers are no more attentive to the child's emotional and developmental difficulties.

The caseworkers, however, are not the source of these in-house problems. Without central control, with guidelines left unspecified, uncommunicated, and unenforced, how can staff be expected to provide health care in a coherent manner? The disorganization pervading the agencies is to blame for this situation. With the agencies in disarray, responsibility for supervising the care of the child is handed down again, as far as it can go (unless the child is expected to monitor his own health needs), to the foster parents. Perhaps this is as it should be. Perhaps it is the duty of the foster parents, who have volunteered their homes and who receive a stipend for the child, to take over the child's health care. However, the children are still a public charge, and some oversight body still should be responsible for ensuring that the foster parents are equipped and willing to provide adequate health care.

Foster parents typically are not self-assured regarding health care. The low socioeconomic status and education levels common among foster parents have been correlated with haphazard health maintenance. Often these parents are incorrect in their perceptions of their foster child's health. Ninety-four percent of the survey mothers regarded their child's present health as good or excellent, a statistic that is not consistent with the findings of the evaluators. If foster parents who are initially not comfortable or perceptive in dealing with health care are to be certified, they must be educated. However, when foster mothers were asked about receiving pre-

ventive health information from the agencies, more than half said they had
received no material, and the majority had not been provided at the time of
placement with information on the medical history of the child. This lack of
information often means that the mother presumes the child to be well and
discovers only later that physical or emotional problems exist.

Ignorance is hardly the worst problem existing in the foster home as a
result of agency carelessness. Far too often, as stated before, children are
beaten and abused in their new homes. It is amazing that 35 percent of the
abusive foster families are recertified for foster care. Still more astonishing
is the fact that 13 percent of all foster parents involved in reported or con-
firmed abuse cases have been arrested previously and that 5 percent have
had criminal convictions. This situation is inexcusable. How can such risks
be taken with a child's life?

A summary of the foster-care process is as follows: A child is taken
from one impaired family, and responsibility for his or her care is then
passed from state to agency to a foster home that may or may not be
suitable. If the child continues to recieve poor care or have problems in his
foster home, the solution is to place the child in another, possibly worse,
home. Twenty-seven percent of the survey children were placed in more
than one home, and 15 percent had lived with three or more foster families.
This lack of stability has a great impact on a child's mental and physical
health. In spite of their presence within the foster-care system, many children remain transient and uncared for.

To ameliorate this so-called system of foster care, it is not enough to
make it coherent. The real system exists in the sense of a workable structure
that provides health care for foster children. Each level in the hierarchy
and, to an extent, each individual entity in the system exists in greater or
lesser isolation. The foster child's needs slip through the gaps between these
levels. What is necessary is a channel of communication and supervision
between the government body, the agency, and the foster parents. The communication dysjunction and confusion regarding standards must be recti-
fied by the responsible parties.

At the top, the state must set and enforce explicit guidelines for the
agencies. It is futile to urge an agency to administer physical checkups so
many times a year or to recommend that agencies hire certain staff if no one
from the governmental body oversees such matters.

Once guidelines are set, the agencies must meet them. In addition, the
agencies must take responsibility for coordinating their own services. They
must establish in-house guidelines and standards and distribute these to
staff; they must educate their staff and make sure that caseworkers are
aware of the child's physical and psychological needs; they must keep better
records and use them assiduously; and they must keep a closer watch on the
local practitioners used by the foster children.

Communication between the agency and the foster parents is essential. First, the foster parents must be informed of the health status of the child. Beyond that, the agency must ensure that the foster family feels comfortable with the health-care system. This could be accomplished by educating the parents in an accessible, meaningful way. Parents could be invited to group meetings at the agency, but is imperative that transportation be provided if the agency is inconveniently located and that the instruction not be steeped in witless jargon or college-level English. If necessary, translators should be provided. One way or another, parents must be made aware of the importance of their child's health.

The same can be said about the care provided, or recommended, by the agency. It should be accessible and personal. A poorly educated foster mother, who has perhaps been misunderstood or ignored in the past, will resign herself quickly to limiting the care of her child if the practitioners she dealt with are hurried or bombastic. Thus, the agency must ensure sensitive care.

Finally, there comes a point at which responsibility must rest with the foster parent. No matter what their reasons for taking the child, and no matter how poorly they are treated by supervising organizations and physicians, there is no excuse for their ignoring the child's needs. If a child is neglected or abused, the foster parents should not be exonerated but simply never trusted with the care of another child. The agency has no right to gamble with a child's life.

A child has only one childhood in which to grow. Every child has problems during that time, but foster children, because of circumstances in their natural homes, may be more susceptible to the inevitable difficulties of growing up. Indeed, they may be handicapped from the start. An abused or ill child cannot cope as easily with social or academic pressures, with the basic process of maturing. The task of the foster-care system is to strengthen that child, to help him cope, to make him able.

Constant reminders that these children are desperate for care are imperative. We hope that this book will serve as such a reminder because if the responsibility of foster care is not met, the tragedy not only will be the child's but also the nation's. Minds and bodies will be lost irretrievably, misplaced amidst scattered papers, unseen by eyes turned away.

Note

1. D. Fanshel and E.B. Shinn, *Children in Foster Care: A Longitudinal Investigation* (New York: Columbia University Press, 1978).

Index

About the Authors

Florence Kavaler, M.D., is a professor of preventive medicine at the State University of New York, Downstate Medical Center, Brooklyn, New York. She was formerly Assistant Surgeon General of the U.S. Public Health Service and director of the U.S. Public Health Service at Staten Island, New York. Dr. Kavaler was the study director for the Milbank Memorial Fund Commission for the Study of Higher Education for Public Health and was the assistant commissioner for Health and Medical Insurance Programs of the New York City Health Department.

Dr. Kavaler was educated at Barnard College and the State University of New York, Downstate, and has graduate degrees from Columbia University School of Public Health and Administrative Medicine. Her extensive list of publications relates to medical-care evaluation in multiple settings, administrative public-policy dynamics, and reports of research activities in the fields of drug addiction, hospital cost control, aging, and others.

Margaret R. Swire received the B.S. and M.A. in psychology from Columbia University. A health care consultant with New York Health Research Associates, she specializes in the design and implementation of evaluative investigations. She is a former director of the foster-child health study funded by the Maternal and Child Health Service of the U.S. Department of Health, Education and Welfare. Prior to that she devised and conducted research for the New York City Department of Health on various health issues, including cost control and quality of health care in different types of medical-care facilities. She was also director of a professional examination utilization study at the Professional Examination Service of the American Public Health Association, and she has served on the staff of the American Health Foundation of New York City. Her publications include articles on child health issues and health evaluation research that have appeared in a number of professional journals.